Ten Powerf
That Will In

THE POWER OF TEN -

Extraordinary Stories of Ten Top Business Women

Authored by:

THE 2008 TOP TEN BUSINESS WOMEN

of the American Business Women's Association

Cover Design: Lina Lawson

Published in the United States by Serey/Jones Publishers, Inc.
for ABWA Top Ten Business Women

soft cover edition
ISBN: 1-881276-09-0

Printed in the United States on acid free paper.

TABLE OF CONTENTS

FOREWORD

In sharing inspirational stories about members' successes, I've have found that most people enjoy them and more readily understand the points I'm trying to make. The anecdotes and illustrations in this book make it come alive.

This book speaks for itself regarding the very special Top Ten sisterhood. To be selected to this prestigious group, a woman must understand not only how to do something, but have the courage to step outside her comfort zone — repeatedly — and often when she looks back, she is astonished by just how far she has come. Perhaps their stories will encourage you to take that first step toward your next accomplishment.

What makes a successful woman? What sets one apart from another? Often, the only thing keeping a woman from triumph is her self-confidence. Too many women see themselves as lacking the credentials they need to compete with others. There is a tacit assumption among some that impossible things in life can only be accomplished by someone special, smarter, richer, poorer or better educated — as if there were a race of superior beings on earth. In fact, extraordinary accomplishments are often made by ordinary people. The women featured in the following pages know there is no point in waiting for someone with "superior qualifications" to do a job. They are confident enough to just step in and do it. They are good role models who inspire others to be strong, self-reliant and well-defined women. As mentors, they are treasures beyond price! Long before David Letterman made Top Ten lists part of the vernacular; the American Business Women's Association was compiling some impressive lists of its own. Since the early 1950s, ABWA has recognized ten members each year for exceptional achievements. These special women have excelled in meeting career goals and enhancing their educations. They give back to their communities and are committed to the mission of ABWA. Top Tens also strive to achieve a balance in their careers, their personal activities and their families. The Top Ten Businesswomen of ABWA represent our Association's image of achievement as well as that of our culture — and serve as the personification of success not only for our members, but women everywhere.

Carolyn B. Elman
Chief Executive Officer
American Business Women's Association

The ABWA Top Ten Business Women

The American Business Women's Association is a national organization founded in 1949 for the purpose of supporting women in the workplace. Today ABWA is one of the preeminent groups representing working women, numbering approximately 40,000 members throughout the United States. The mission statement of ABWA is:

To bring together businesswomen of diverse occupations and to provide opportunities for them to help themselves and others grow personally and professionally through leadership, education, networking support and national recognition.

The Top Ten Business Women award is an honor bestowed each year upon ten ABWA members from across the nation in recognition of outstanding achievement. Recipients are selected based upon their achievements in education, career, community service and service to local chapters of ABWA. The Top Tens represent the Association's image of success and serve as important role models for members.

The 2008 Top Tens are a uniquely diverse group of business women, having earned their distinction in a variety of fields and through unusual career paths. Most have excelled in their careers while negotiating personal challenges which would have derailed many women not exhibiting their strength of character and persistence. Their stories are widely divergent, but all are united through their efforts to support other working women, and their common bond as members of ABWA.

8/17/08

Julie Kangas
2008 American Business Woman of ABWA

The proceeds of the sales of this book will assist other women in attaining their educational and career goals. The ABWA scholarship programs will benefit from your support.

The 2008 ABWA Top Tens

Honoring the 2008 Top Ten Business Women of ABWA

The prestigious Top Ten Business Women of ABWA award was presented to ten outstanding members of the American Business Women's Association at the 2007 National Women's Leadership Conference in Greensboro, N.C. This annual award, which has been presented by the Association since 1956, recognizes ten members from across the country for outstanding achievement in their careers, community involvement and professional development. Among the Top Ten, one woman is chosen as the American Business Woman of ABWA. Those who are selected represent ABWA during a year of travel, public speaking and mentoring.

The winners of this year's Top Ten Business Women of ABWA were selected for their many career and philanthropic achievements, as well as for their ability to demonstrate how their involvement in the Association has contributed directly to significant career achievements.

A panel of independent judges for the 2008 Top Ten Business Women award selected the following women, who have all been active in ABWA at the local or national level.

2008 American Business Woman of ABWA

Dr. Julie Kangas

Escondido, California

Soaring Eagles Chapter

Dentist/Owner, Citracado Dental Group

Julie, a dentist and owner of the Citracado Dental Group, says that keeping her business running efficiently on all levels requires great leadership and delegation skills. Her goals include improving her leadership skills, as well as increasing the size of her business and adding new services to her dental practice. Within the next several years, she plans to either begin a dental practice management certificate program, or retain the services of a professional business coach.

"ABWA has had a significant part in helping me to clarify and work toward my goals," she says. "Of primary importance have been the friendships and professional relationships of the members of my chapter, the Soaring Eagles. Many of my ABWA colleagues are small business owners like myself and face the same types of challenges I deal with on a regular basis. We all must build our own businesses by finding and keeping clients, managing our finances and creating a business structure and culture that will fuel growth and help us stay focused on our goals. My leadership roles in ABWA have helped me increase my business knowledge and provide a way to help other women also."

Tina Ackles
Killeen, Texas
Globe Chapter
Associate, Booz Allen Hamilton

Now an associate for Booz Allen Hamilton in Killeen, Texas, Tina's previous work required that she serve as a field software engineer, working on military bases across the U.S., Korea and Germany. A portion of Tina's work has been to provide technical support and on-site training to military intelligence soldiers.

Voted Woman of the Year for the Globe Chaper in 2005, Tina says her goals include reaching the Inner Circle, a special ABWA recognition given to those members who have sponsored eleven or more new members. "I really want to share the ABWA experience with as many women as possible," she says.

Prior to joining the Association, Tina says one of her goals was to become active in a worthwhile organization in the business world. "As fate would have it, my Veteran's Affairs counselor was a member of ABWA. She invited me to a meeting and I was immediately hooked. I went to my first spring conference three weeks later," Tina says, adding that, "In addition, I received an SBMEF grant for my graduate work. Having completed many continuing education credits through ABWA and through my various committee and board assignments, I have greatly improved my leadership skills and public speaking skills. I was able to submit my CEU credits to our corporate training officer and have them added to my training file. I believe this helped me secure my latest promotion."

Janet I. Deyette
Deltona, Florida
Four Townes Charter Chapter
Tax Accountant/Real Estate Broker-Associate/Co-owner;
Tri County Financial Services

A tax accountant/real estate broker-associate and co-owner of Tri County Financial Services, Janet says over the next five years she plans to continue building her business so that it can be sold outright, or take in an associate so that she can semi-retire.

Elected to a four-year term as a city commissioner in 2005, Janet credits ABWA's training for her gaining the confidence to start a new chapter in her life in such a role. Janet says that prior to ABWA she was uncomfortable speaking in public and she knew little about how to organize a fundraiser. But in 2005, at the age of 67, "I had the audacity to run for office for the first time in my life," she says. "I knew my husband and my ABWA sisters would be rooting for me – just as they do for each and every one of us who reaches out beyond our comfort zones," she explains.

"Speaking at ABWA meetings had helped immensely with my speaking ability. I discovered that running a political campaign wasn't much different from organizing and putting on a fundraiser. The Four Townes Art Auctions and the Great GiveAway Events held each year provided fantastic training ground. My campaign strategies all came together and I won by over 62 percent of the vote.

"The friendship, support, camaraderie and just plain fun-times together with ABWA members cannot be measured," she says.

Dr. Rebecca Pulliam Francis
Smithfield, North Carolina
Johnston Charter Chapter
Instructor/Coordinator-Basic Skills ILC
Wake Technical Community College

A self-described advocate of life-long learning, Rebecca's professional goal is to someday be the president of a community college. Currently an instructor/coordinator in the Individualized Learning Center at Wake Technical Community College in Raleigh, N.C., Rebecca says that by taking on such a role, she would have a "real opportunity for making a difference for adults of all ages and backgrounds through education."

Rebecca says that she recently took another step toward accomplishing her goal by earning her Doctorate of Education in Higher Education Administration from North Carolina State University in Raleigh, N.C. A Johnston Charter Chapter member, she has held the roles of chapter president, vice-president, secretary, treasurer and chapter advisor, among others.

"Much of the credit for the development of my leadership and team building skills, I give to my nineteen years in ABWA," Francis says. "The Johnston Charter Chapter has served as a safe incubator to learn and practice leadership skills. The chapter and national organization have provided friendships and a network to support my personal growth, self-confidence and communication skills."

Christina Robinson Grochett
The Woodlands, Texas
Houston Area Professional Express Network
Campus Director
University of Phoenix- Houston Campuses

Since joining ABWA in 1997, Christina says that the chief benefit she has received from the Association has been the encouragement to believe that her success is only limited by what she believes she can accomplish. In addition she states, "I am strongly committed to helping women believe that they can succeed and dare to achieve their goals and to bring women together who feel the same. Because of the direct benefits realized by me, I encourage women to join ABWA and experience the personal growth available to them."

A member of the Houston Area Professional Express Network in Houston, Texas, Christina is a campus director for the University of Phoenix – Houston Campuses. She says support from ABWA members gave her the confidence to run for president of the first Express Network in her district, as well as president of the Houston Area Council of ABWA. She adds, "The American Business Women's Association, through the members and programs, provides one with the knowledge and a support network needed to achieve whatever one desires. The women of ABWA have given me a support network and provided me with role models and mentors. These mentors have enriched my personal and professional life significantly. I find it hard to imagine my life without ABWA. I know I would not be where I am today managing a university without the confidence ABWA and the women who manage it have given me."

Richie B. Morris
Stone Mountain, Georgia
Hidden Hills Chapter
Contractor, Delta Airlines

A desire to help others has been a driving force for Richie throughout her career, and continues to propel her into her next adventure. With a background in sociology and psychology, she's decided to take her helping spirit to the next level with a doctorate in geriatrics. "I am passionate about learning and sharing and have always been deeply compassionate toward the elderly. A doctorate degree would not only quench my thirst for learning but it would provide greater tools for me to serve."

That same serving spirit is also part of her ABWA experience. "Helping ABWA members achieve their goals is very rewarding and I have also known how wonderful it is to make phone calls or write emails and have members drop their plans and immediately come to my rescue when needed. ABWA has given me a huge network of clients, supporters and mentors. I am fully qualified and equipped to succeed, thanks to ABWA."

Marcita Scharnhorst

Douglasville, Georgia

Douglas County Charter Chapter

Vice President of Human Resources, GreyStone Power Corporation

The Vice President of Human Resources is expected to do many things, including leading and speaking in front of groups, overseeing human resources program and supervising staff. For Marcita, that important role was punctuated with the additional responsibility of being the first female executive staff member since the corporation was formed nearly 75 years ago. She turned to her experience within ABWA to sharpen the skills she needed to perform her best.

"My thirteen years of ABWA leadership training and skills development prepared me to have the ability and self-confidence to handle the tasks that were given to me by my manager, the President/CEO of GreyStone Power. He saw me as an officer and leader of ABWA. I earned the privilege to become a member of the management team. ABWA gave me the ability to speak in front of groups and to have the self-confidence in my ability to lead and direct people. I can accomplish anything that I decide I want to tackle."

"ABWA is the only professional organization that I found that allows me to grow friendships and allows me to develop skills and talents that I never knew I had. ABWA has far exceeded my expectations of giving back to me personally far more than I ever anticipated that I would gain from this organization."

Diana Morales Taylor
Kingwood, Texas
Humble Artesian Chapter, Humble, Texas
CEO, YWCA Greater Houston

An advocate for women and minorities, Diana serves as the CEO of the YWCA Greater Houston and has dedicated her career to issues that affect these groups. When she joined ABWA, she found that same dedication within her group and its members.

"Women's empowerment and development have been the mainstays of both my professional and personal life for many years. When I was approached for membership into ABWA, I was intrigued by the cross-section of careers, professions and jobs that were represented within the chapter. Increasing the economic empowerment of women has been a personal goal of my adult life. Of course, membership in ABWA was a natural fit for me. "

An avid lifelong learner, Diana hopes to parley her interest in social issues into additional studies in sociology, social work and non-profit management. "The focus on education that ABWA exhibits firmly aligns with my personal commitment to the value of education. At each meeting the focus on educational development is clear. Whether it is the national magazine or our chapter speakers, ABWA, as I do, understands that the quickest path to self sufficiency and resilience is education."

Katreena Hayes-Wood
Glendale, Arizona
Arrowhead Millennium Chapter
President/Owner, STRIVE for STUDENTS

Love what you do. That's how Katreena sums up career, involvement in ABWA and her life – and she has a passion for them all.

The owner of STRIVE for STUDENTS, Katreena's business was the result of her personal dedication to young people in her area – including her own son – who needs support for finding a career.

"I have dedicated my 22-year career to helping people discover career success by showing them how to define their career purpose. As a career development specialist, I have led my company, STRIVE for STUDENTS, to create dynamic and successful career-related workshops, program materials and web-based tools."

While charting a career path for others is a goal, Katreena also found her own career success in the support of her fellow members.

"Through my association with my ABWA friends, I was inspired to write my book, *Help! I Need a Job.* I co-authored a second book called *Dream Circles: How to Make Your Dreams Come True Through the Power of Sharing*. My ABWA friend and co-author had the idea from attending a power brunch with ABWA friends."

Christine F. Wright
Cape Coral, Florida
Cape Coral Caloosa Chapter
President/Attorney, Wright & Shaw, P.A.

Professionalism is paramount for attorney and chapter president, Christine. In both her career and her association with ABWA, she believes in maintaining a professional attitude.

"As president of the chapter, I have led the group to a more professional level, encouraging more professionalism and camaraderie among the members. This has resulted in many chapter members not only participating in the chapter activities, but also an increase in the number of members attending the local, district and national events."

As a businesswoman, Christine looks to her fellow members for support, and is always happy to provide that support when needed as well.

"I joined ABWA shortly after opening my own practice. My chapter members have been an invaluable source of support, information, advice and guidance as my business has blossomed. We are fortunate to have a diversified membership, and I have been able to look toward my fellow members when needing a service from a particular business for myself, or one of my clients."

Tina Ackles

I'll never forget the day I found out that I had been voted one of the 2008 Top Ten Businesswomen of ABWA. I had taken a new job with Booz Allen Hamilton and was in New Jersey for training.

Late one evening I was checking email and saw one from Robin Necci, the current ABWA National President. Robin and I had met several years ago at Spring Conference and become instant friends. I read the email and thought she had been voted one of this year's Top Tens. I instantly responded with congratulations. I was so excited for her.

The next day I received a reply from Robin. In short she said, "Hey, YOU are the Top Ten!! Call me on my cell!!"

Now I was really excited. I called Robin and we talked for a few minutes. I was so honored and humbled to learn that I was to join the Top Ten family. They are such an amazing group of women.

A couple of days later I received the assignment from national that I was to give a three minute speech at the national convention. The topic was Servant Leadership. I was to talk about someone outside of my family who had been a servant leader to me. This was an easy task for me. I knew exactly who I would talk about — Ms. Martha Cessna, my home economics teacher from high school.

Now for those who know me well, this is probably laughable. For those who don't, allow me to explain. I took four years of home economics in high school. In addition, I was in the Future Homemakers of America (FHA). I was actually president my senior year. Why is this so ironic? I don't cook or sew. I think my stove was used twice last year. You know how there are those who make crafts and those who buy? I am definitely a buyer, but not due to lack of training.

In addition to teaching, Ms. Cessna was a mentor. I was born and raised in Greenville, Kentucky, a town of about 6,000 with one stoplight at the time. There was not a lot of industry in our town so options were limited. Most girls grew up to marry local boys and raise families. But Ms. Cessna taught us that we could do whatever we set our minds to. We were not limited to the boundaries of Greenville; the world was our oyster. I don't know how many times over those four years she told me, "You can do anything!"

And in the background was my mom, Brenda, telling me to live my life for myself before I settled down to be a mother and wife because being a mom is a lifetime commitment of putting others first, so I should do something for myself and live my own life before making that commitment. And I listened.

I graduated from high school and continued working in a local fast food restaurant. One day while I was working the drive-thru I focused on one of my co-workers. She was 35 years old, (ancient to me at the time) and working the counter. All I knew was that I did not want to be standing behind that counter at 35 — not that there is anything wrong with the job. It's just really hard work for very little pay.

So when I was approached by an Army recruiter a month later, I was open to the ideas he presented. Army recruiters are salesmen and he gave a great pitch. The best of it was that the Army would help me with my dream of going to college. I didn't know about grants and loans at the time so I felt college was beyond my reach. The Army could make that dream a reality, the recruiter told me. I was sold, but we had to convince my dad.

I told the recruiter to really focus on the college benefits when he spoke to my dad. Even though I was 19 and could make the decision for myself, I wanted my dad's blessing. And he gave it. Three days later I was on a bus to Louisville to process in.

There were a lot of job options to choose from, but when I read about being a chaplain's assistant, I thought that was the one for me. I knew that my parents would be more comfortable with my leaving if I was in a job that they felt was safe. So I signed up. I had three months until my report day. During that time I couldn't even count the number of people who didn't really believe I would go.

I remember going back to school and telling Ms. Cessna.

As always she was supportive and told me she knew I could do it. And I did. I completed basic training in Alabama, finished Advanced Individual Training (AIT) in New Jersey, and then I headed to Germany for my first assignment.

A lot of people asked me if I was scared. I was 19, on my own for the first time and heading to a country where I didn't even speak the language. Was I scared? That's an understatement. But I had made a commitment. My clearest memory was the train ride from Frankfurt to Garmisch. Having never been on a train before, I didn't realize that several of the cars would be dropped in Garmisch and the remaining would continue on to Austria. Just my luck I was on one of the cars that would continue to Austria. I was sitting across from an elderly German couple who attempted to talk to me. I couldn't understand them and they couldn't understand me, so I just said Garmisch since it was the only word I was sure they would understand. They smiled and nodded their heads enthusiastically. And for the remaining two hours of the trip when our eyes met they'd smile and say Garmisch.

I noticed the train only paused for about two minutes at each stop, and I was worried about getting my duffle bags off the train in time. Those who know me know I never pack light. I didn't even realize we were in Garmisch until the elderly gentleman started throwing my duffels off the train. And we made it with seconds to spare. They stood in the doorway smiling and waving until the train was out of sight. I was in Germany.

I spent a year in Garmisch and a year in Karlsruhe, and I learned a lot — enough to fill up several chapters, but I'll limit it to this. There were good things and bad things. I was a child in an adult world; I realized I had lived a very sheltered life, so some of the lessons were harder to take than others. But I persevered. And I was able to see Europe, something I never ever dreamed I'd do.

One of the main things I realized was that I was not cut out to be a chaplain's assistant. It was a nice, easy job, but not challenging. In Garmisch there was a Russian institute where military officers came to study the Russian language. Since I was up for re-enlistment, I decided I wanted to become a Russian linguist. Several people have asked me "why Russian?"

And my answer was because of the challenge. I figured high school kids learn Spanish, German, French and I wanted something a little more difficult. I had joined the Army for the college benefits, but I was enjoying the adventure. So I took the required test and complete the application to transfer. I left Germany for Fort McClellan, Alabama and waited for the application process to play out.

I admit, at times I can be stubborn. The re-enlistment officer said the application required me to select three languages and the Army would choose for me. To which I responded with Russian, Russian, and Russian. I explained that if I was going to dedicate a year of my life learning a language it would need to be one that I was interested in learning. The officer said that approach would limit my options, but I took the chance. I knew I could always leave the Army and go to college. But with a 50 percent failure rate among its personnel studying Russian, I was sure the Army would allow me to study it. Heck, they needed all the help they could get.

A year later I found myself at the Defense Language Institute in Monterrey, California studying Russian. It was an intense 47-week program. We had physical training in the morning, and then six hours a day in the classroom studying one subject. You'd think it would become boring after a while, but it never did. I loved it and I found I had an aptitude for languages, which I am sad to say, upset my roommate who studied for at least three hours each evening, while I spent the time hanging out with my friends then frantically studied for 10 minutes each morning before the quizzes.

We had weekends off to enjoy the West Coast, from L.A. to San Francisco. It was an exciting year. Then it was off to Goodfellow Air Force Base, in San Angelo, Texas to complete my training.

After graduating, I received orders again for Germany to Berlin, home of Field Station Berlin, a highly desired strategical assignment. So a small town Kentucky girl headed to a major European city with a population exceeding three million. It was a cultural shock, to say the least.

Berlin and Garmisch are like New York City and Greenville, worlds apart. I spent the next three years learning: learning the city, learning my job, learning the language. I had the opportunity to see the Berlin Wall and then to see the Berlin Wall fall. To see history, to be a part of it, was an amazing time. But all good things come to an end, and I ended up in Fort Polk, Louisiana.

Now there are many, especially those who have been stationed there, who might groan over this twist of fate, but I did not. I have always felt that life is what you make of it. I had learned that from the previous assignments. I knew people in Berlin who never left the military base, never went downtown, never traveled to East Berlin or to West Germany. There's even a name for someone like that — a barrack's rat. So when I arrived in Louisiana it was with an open mind, and I spent the next three years doing what I do best — learning. Learning a new unit, learning a new job, learning how to make fun out of nothing, because there is literally nothing in Leesville, Louisiana.

The most wonderful thing that came out of my time in Louisiana is my best friend, Marlene. We met in 1991. I was dating a nice guy who wanted to introduce me to his best friend. I was a little leery when I found out it was a girl, but luckily I agreed. And that was probably — no, definitely — one of the best decisions I have made in my life. We hit it off immediately. We became best friends and I'm not even sure what happened to the guy or even remember his name. I'm sure Marlene would remember if I asked. But anyway, Marlene moved in with me and when the time came for me to transfer to Fort Hood, Texas, I talked her into moving, too.

We made the move in January of 1993 and never looked back. Before we knew it, we were both dating soldiers from Fort Hood and life was good. Unfortunately, the Army wasn't. I had spent three years on the promotion list and was no closer to getting promoted. The points were high for Russian linguists and I was lacking the 100 points I could get for college credits. I didn't have any college credits. I had spent a lot of time in the field in Louisiana and college wasn't an option. It appeared the same would be true in Fort Hood.

I decided that I would apply to switch languages to Arabic. They were in desperate need of Arabic linguists, but it seemed that Russians were not yet able to leave even though there were no true jobs left for Russian linguists. I mean, who needs a Russian linguist in Texas or Louisiana? I was coming up on 10 years in the military and I had a decision to make. Should I do 10 more or get out and go to school?

It was a tough decision. I loved the old Army but was not too impressed with the new Army. I felt they were holding me back. I wasn't sure I could do another 10 years. My boyfriend, Allen, and I talked about the decision together. So we decided I would get out of the Army and go to college. I left the Army in May of 1993. I applied to the VA for educational benefits and was waiting for the approval process to be completed. I drew unemployment and spent the next three months trying to find a job. I never dreamed it would be so hard. I thought I had some skills. Finally, in August, I paid a headhunter firm to find me a job. I started working as a warranty clerk at the local Ford dealership.

It was definitely different being a civilian again, but I was learning a new job. I even helped to get Marlene hired by the dealership as an assistant in service. In November, Allen and I were married. Marlene moved on to cashier and I moved on to service advisor. But it was long hours and little pay. So in February 1995 I took a job as a data collector for a contractor at Fort Hood. It was a temporary position, but the pay was better and there was opportunity to continue from one contract to another. At the end of the first contract, I was asked to move on to the second. This entailed an eight week stay in Fort Sill, Oklahoma. Allen and I were still discussing this, and much to our surprise I found out that same week that I was pregnant.

We had been trying to have a baby for the previous two years. I had even gone through infertility surgery and artificial insemination, but nothing had worked. So six months prior we had essentially given up hope and accepted the fact that there would be no children. So when I started feeling ill, I assumed I'd caught the flu. When I was tired, I assumed it was from working shift work again and adjusting to the time changes. But then, Easter Sunday, I figured it out. We bought a pregnancy test, then another, and we were finally convinced. We were going to have a baby. It was the happiest moment of my life up to that point.

Then I received my approval from the VA for my college program. It was too good to be true —baby and a college degree. I started college in August. Our son, Christopher, was born December 1st, two and a half weeks early. I was not ready.

I was studying for my first finals. I hadn't even bought the crib sheets yet. But there he was, and that was the happiest moment of my life. A week and a half later, I took the finals on schedule. And that was the last easy semester. It's challenging juggling a baby and college education, and when Christopher was eight months old, I went back to work part-time. We couldn't afford to live on just Allen's Army pay, so I became a substitute teacher. I worked on the days I didn't have classes. Then Allen came up on orders to Korea.

So for the next year it was just Christopher and I. Oh, and the house, and the job, and dog, and the lawn, and the bills, and the classes, and the homework. It was a long year.

Then Allen returned. I graduated from Central Texas College, the junior college, and continued on to the University of Central Texas. I applied for a work-study position in the VA office at the university and began that job in August of 1997. It was a good arrangement, because it was a part time position that worked around my classes. And I could do my homework at work when we weren't busy.

In my last semester, I applied for an intern position as a computer programmer at McLane Company in Temple, Texas. This was to fulfill a college course and would allow me to get some experience in the computer industry. During the interview, I was offered a full-time position with the company. I accepted on the condition that I would be able to leave work to complete my remaining courses. During this time, my VA representative, Candy, invited me to attend an ABWA meeting. I really enjoyed it and I joined that night, and three weeks later attended my first spring conference. I was blown away. I met such an exceptional group of women, and it was a very motivating experience.

I graduated a few months later with my Bachelor's of Science in computer science with a minor in business administration — I am proud to say with a 4.0 GPA. It was a lot of hard work, but I had finally realized my dream of becoming a college graduate. And now I had new dreams.

I wanted to become more involved in my ABWA chapter. Well, that's all they had to hear. I was selected to be the ways and means chair for the upcoming year. I was a little worried to start, but everyone was so supportive. It went so well that I volunteered to fill the position for a second year. Things were going smoothly.

Now that I was working full-time, Allen left the military to pursue his degree in accounting. In April 2000, I was offered a position as a field software engineer for L3 Communications/ ILEX Systems. It was working as a government contractor on Fort Hood supporting military intelligence computer systems and the soldiers who use them. I was doing well at McLane's, but I was working in a cubicle. I missed the variety and adventure of the Army. So I was happy to make the change. Actually, it was like coming home. I spent time in the field with the soldiers, traveled to California with them for exercises, and it was interesting work.

My life changed drastically in 2001. Allen and I separated. It was a tough time for everyone, especially Christopher. I will never forget the day Allen moved out, and the look on my son's face. He was five years old, and his reaction broke my heart.

Thankfully, I had my ABWA sisters for support. I had run for treasurer and it was just the distraction I need to get through. In 2002, Allen and I divorced. It was as amicable as any divorce can be, I guess. We both agreed that the most important thing was that Christopher have a good childhood, and happy memories. And we were committed to that. We still are.

Life went on. I ran for treasurer again the following year. And then the year after that for vice-president.

And then things changed again. The war became a reality and Fort Hood was destined to go. And in July 2003, so was I.

Many ask, why? Well, because it was my job. I supported the systems that the military intelligence soldiers would be using to fight the war. I supported the soldiers. It was something I had to do. It was hard on my son, who was seven years old. But thankfully, Allen moved back into the house so our son didn't have to leave his room, or his school.

I deployed to Baghdad for the first two months and then moved to Baquobah for the final four. My chapter supported me with letters, email and packages. I was never far from home.

It was an experience like no other. There are so many stories to tell, but the one I remember most vividly happened on November 20, 2003. I was lying on my cot in my tent reading. I heard the mortar hit and fell to the floor. I struggled into my vest and helmet as the next two mortars landed. Debris hit my tent so I knew they were close. Too close. While the tents have sandbags about waist high around them, there is no overhead protection. So you lie there on the floor hoping nothing hits dead center. When there was a lull, I left the tent to run to the bunker. I couldn't see for all the dirt in the air, and it was so thick you could wave it away with your hand. I will never forget the smell of sulfur. I slid down in to the bunker as more rounds arrived. And a contractor next to me asked, "What are we doing here?"

His hand shook while he lit a cigarette. My knees were literally knocking. I have heard the expression, but now I truly know what it means.

13 were injured, but thankfully no one died that day. And that's just one day. So when my time came and I was asked if I would extend, I said no. Six months was enough.

I returned to my home, my son, and my life, forever changed — and forever grateful for all the things I have in my life, for the freedoms my son enjoys. I continued to grow, to learn, to support my ABWA chapter as they supported me. In 2004, my chapter nominated me for Top Ten. I was proud to be nominated, but never expected to win. In 2005, I ran for vice president again. And I was Globe Chapter Woman of the Year for 2005. What an honor that was.

Then February 2006, I returned to Iraq. I went for a six month rotation to Baghdad. I was due to return in August.

Globe Chapter vice president is actually a president-elect. We like the person to commit to two years on the board. And I was committed. But my company requested that I stay an additional 90 days on the contract. It was a new program and the current program was on its way out. It was a tough decision. I had my son and my chapter to think about. I talked to my son about it and he seemed okay with it. So I had to address the chapter. I had already asked my friend, Debbie, to run for vice president while I ran for president and she had grudgingly agreed. Now I had to convince her to run for president. I knew she could do it. But she was not so sure. With a little encouragement and lot of pushing, she agreed. And she did a fantastic job. I extended a second time and ended up spending a full year in Baghdad. I am hopeful that it is my last.

I ran for vice president again this past year. I guess the third time is a charm. Suprisingly, Debbie wanted to be president a second year. Again, she demonstrated that we never know what we are capable of doing until we give it a try.

My chapter nominated me for Top Ten and for Bell County Area Council Hall of Fame. And in August I took the new job and ended up in Jersey, where this story began. I was inducted into the Hall of Fame. What a year for me this has been!

The National convention in Greensboro was amazing. I

saw many old friends and met many new ones, including my 2008 Top Ten sisters. Someone came up with the idea that we write a book in which we were to share our journeys.

We have all traveled different paths, through different times, to arrive at the same place in time — standing on a stage in Greensboro, North Carolina. We are a diverse group of women, as I am sure you can see. We each have our own views, opinions and beliefs. But through it all we have one thing in common — our membership in the greatest women's organization in the world.

When I look at those who have gone before me, I am humbled to be included in such an outstanding group of women. When I share that with others, they say, "But you are amazing!"

I don't see it that way. I am not a business owner, a CEO, a lawyer, a doctor, a judge, a president or vice-president of a corporation, or a professor. So, for those of you, who like me, thought that qualifications like this are what it takes to become an ABWA Top Ten, think again. I am living proof that it's not about a title or position — it's about the person.

It's about who you are and what you believe in. The joke around work is that I represent the little man, or woman, but that doesn't sound the same. I cannot believe the number of people who have come up to me and congratulated me on being named to the ABWA Top Ten. Okay, so it helps that the local paper ran a big story about it in the business section. But it still astonishes me and I find it hard to believe I have come this far

If I could pinpoint the one thing that I think has led to my success, it would be the work ethic that I was taught by my dad, Dareld — to give 110 percent to whatever task is at hand. Whether you like that task or not is irrelevant, it's the effort you put into it that matters. And others notice this.

As a result of my implementation of that simple lesson, my career has continued to progress. I must admit I received an evaluation once that said I should not expect others' work ethics to be as high as mine or I would always be disappointed and frustrated. I responded, "Are you saying I should lower my work ethic? Not in this lifetime."

So to those of you reading this, remember — you can do anything, be anything. It's all up to you. And if you can believe in yourself, just half as much as others believe in you, you can do wondrous things.

And finally, be thankful for all that we have in this country and remember those who gave and are still giving their lives so that we can live ours.

Janet I. Deyette

My father used to tell me, "You can be anything you want to be. Reach for the stars." My father also loved to practice random acts of kindness. He set an example I could not forget. And he believed whatever you do should be fun. Though he has passed from this life, his words and actions have stayed in my mind and continue to encourage me and guide me.

I was born in Hartford, Connecticut. But my memories of childhood really began when my father's job took us to the Buffalo, New York area. I remember the trip in our tiny silver house trailer with Mom trying to keep the dishes from falling out of the cabinets and Dad's customer watches swinging on the pegboard where they hung. We lived in a trailer park for a while, and then moved from rental to rental in suburban towns with names like Cheektowaga and Ebenezer, until my parents were able to purchase a 150 year old home on two acres to call their own. For the first time in our lives we experienced life without indoor plumbing. In winter we shoveled a path to the outhouse before going to bed.

My four younger brothers and I grew up on that little two-acre "farm" in Depew, New York that played a huge part in developing our imaginations. The little thicket of a forest became our own Tarzan's jungle. We used our Lone Ranger and Tonto handbooks and learned to lash twigs and tree limbs together and construct bridges and rafts for the creek. A horse-crazy tomboy of a girl back then, I would catch the huge draft horses in the farmers' pastures, tie strings to the halters and ride, and imagine all sorts of wonderful adventures. We played all day in the outdoors during the summer, ate apples off the trees and cow corn from the fields. In the winter storms we played Sergeant Preston of the Yukon, and we tried to get our poor little dog to pull a sled.

When my Dad and uncle finally installed running water, it was necessary to dig a tunnel under the kitchen to run pipes to the bathroom and over to the kitchen sink. We lucky kids could now boast that our home had a secret tunnel. Much later my parents told us we were rather poor during those years. But we never knew it. We always had enough to eat because of the family garden. We five provided part of the assembly line to can fruits and vegetables to last through the long winters.

We were rich in imagination and filled with a zest for

adventure. I never felt defeated. I dreamed of future success. At Christmas we would list a few main gifts we hoped to receive. My heart was filled with excitement upon opening my first pair of ice skates. It was the only thing I'd asked for. I put them on and kept trying, and falling, getting up, and falling again, until I was finally able to stay up, build speed, and feel the cold wind stinging my eyes. This was the life, the spirit, and the grounding that gave me courage and an attitude for keeping on that carried me forward on this journey toward the Top Ten award.

My Journey as a Parent

I married in 1958. My husband was drafted into the Army three months later. Six months after that I was able to join him near the base, where we lived for a year-and-a-half. Our identical twin boys, Chester Jr. and Clifford, were born in 1959 at the Army hospital on the base in Fort Knox, Kentucky. Shortly after leaving the Army, we bought a 56 acre farm in Akron, New York. This was the opportunity to realize my dreams of raising horses on my own farm. We named it Creekside Farm and I chose green and white as my show colors. I bred, trained and showed Morgan horses. For ten years my life revolved around the children, my husband, and the horses. Raising twin boys was a bit traumatic, so I waited nine years to try for a girl. Our third son, Clayton was born in 1968. The twins were fascinated with their little brother and took turns helping with him. Our boys had the advantage of spending their early years in a wholesome country environment, as I had, but with indoor plumbing.

My husband never shared my passion for the horses. I had tried to get him to ride with me and come to the shows. But he seemed to resent them. I was content. All my childhood dreams of having beautiful horses had come true. I never dreamed life would change. But adversity and change did come. One brood mare got out of the barn and was hit by a car. One hind leg was severed and I had to have her euthanized. The agonizing helplessness I felt will never be forgotten. When race horses, such as Barbaro and then Eight Belles in this year's Derby break down on the track, I relive that awful moment.

My husband began pushing me to sell the horses. And in my sadness, I gave in and sold the others, except for the stallion. He had been the first colt born on our little farm – out in the pasture. I had carried him into the freshly cleaned stall. Deeply thankful, I'd registered him Creekside Blessing, though we nicknamed him "Buddy." Just like in the movies, he came to my whistle. Gentle and loving, yet high-spirited, this beautiful bay colt was the very picture of what the original Morgan horse looked like. He won the blue ribbons at halter and as an excited two-year-old he'd placed third the first time shown in harness. I loved driving him into town with my twin boys on each side of me. This one I could not sell. I donated him to a Christian Campground. Once the horses were gone, the farm lost its charm. A farm devoid of animals was useless and unfulfilling.

We moved to an ordinary house in the suburbs. While living there, the stallion I had donated was returned to me when the campground closed. What a joyful time that was. However, not living on a farm meant we had to incur boarding expenses. This situation strained our budget and our fragile marriage. I finally did sell Buddy to a young couple who promised to use him as a stud and carry on his excellent bloodline. Horses were no longer part of my life at all. I had lost my passion. I later learned that one of the mares I'd sold to a farm in Vermont had been struck by lightning. I had no idea what a different future might lay ahead.

In 1974, we moved to Florida. The grooming skills I had learned on the farm enabled me to open my own dog grooming business. Florida's long hot summer was perfect for fleas and I soon had a booming business in dog hair and flea dip. But it was not easy work and dog hair gets into sinuses. I finally tired of smelling like flea dip and decided to try a cleaner type of work. In 1979, I obtained a real estate license and sold the dog grooming business. During this period of time, my marriage finally failed. In 1982, I became a real estate broker and an instructor, and divorced my husband of 24 years. I spent the next few years selling homes and learning about the commercial end of the profession.

I met my current husband while working in the real estate business. I had no plans to ever marry again. But we soon became good friends. I married Earl "Mac" Deyette on September 3rd in 1984. Life began to change in big ways. I had found a man who, like my father, believed in me, respected me, and encouraged me to reach for my dreams. But when we moved to Deltona in Volusia County the nation was in a recession that had devastated the real estate market. As brokers we were doubly hit and feared losing our own home. My new husband's optimism aroused within me the old ideals I'd learned with my family during the tough times growing up on that little farm.

College Bound at 50+
Turning Adversity into Opportunity

We began to look for ways to survive. First, we moved our real estate operations into a "home office." Then he told me he would "hold the fort," take care of the real estate business, and I would go to college. I had always wanted to attend college but as the oldest of five, my hopes for a college education had been replaced by the need to obtain employment following high school graduation. Later, marriage, children, and horses had filled my life. The day I proudly watched my sons graduate from the University of Central Florida, I remember wondering if I would ever be able to follow in *their* footsteps.

In May of 1993, in the middle of the recession, my husband convinced me that this was the perfect time for me to enter college. We figured I could learn some computer skills and get a job outside of real estate. At the age of 55, I entered college for the first time in my life. My husband was proudly boasting to all who would listen, "I can't afford to retire. I have a wife in college."

From running the horse farm as a business and later the dog grooming shop, I found that I enjoyed business and entrepreneurial challenges. I had also discovered during the recession that competition in the work force had become really tough without some sort of credentials. A wise counselor suggested I build on the knowledge I had already acquired and steered me into accounting, and I plunged ahead. Two years in, I needed to make a critical decision, whether to take the AA degree and go for an entry-level job in accounting or forge on into the scary world of higher learning. Even though I was doing very well in the classes, I still thought I was too old to go for a four-year degree. I was over 50!

It was January of 1995 when I met Dr. Sylvester Covington. Always willing to explore all possibilities, my husband and I were there for my interview to consider transferring as a sophomore into the University of Central Florida (UCF). It was late in the afternoon and the man in the black suit was visibly tired. My husband was boasting to him about how well I'd done and that I had a 4.0 GPA. Dr. Covington straightened up and said, "Wow, sounds like this young lady means business."

He asked several questions about what I liked to do and what I hoped to accomplish with my skills and education so far. He assured me that if I really wanted to have my own accounting business, I could do it. He would show me the way. And over the next two years he did.

I never forgot that man because he was so much more than an advisor or counselor. I later learned he wore many hats. He was the Coordinator of UCF's School of Business at Daytona Beach, Director of Student Advisement, and professor of several management and marketing classes. He was important. This year was important. This was UCF's first year for their launch of BE2000, a new approach to learning by partnering with business owners around the community. This was the year UCF was making its big push to combine business and research with learning by putting student teams to work with companies desiring new ideas and new answers. This was my chance to be a part of that. And for guidance I had Dr. Covington. His style was to lead by serving. We students never realized how well he was leading the way. By serving up whatever guidance was needed all along, he served and he led. He loved to say, "Always ask for what you want – 'cause you just might get it."

I did get it. My journey through college was so exciting and fulfilling that, after earning the B.S. degree in accounting, I continued on for the Master of Business Administration (MBA) with a concentration in Entrepreneurship. I met many wonderful and talented instructors and leaders along the way, but none was ever quite like Dr. Sylvester Covington. That college journey ended in December 2002 with a Master in Human Resources/Change Management.

Meanwhile, all the degrees one collects if you stay in school long enough paid off and my very own taxes and accounting business was growing.

The real estate business, in which my husband had said he'd "hold the fort" until the recession ended, had expanded into commercial management and leasing and included two shopping centers. Now as partners in our own dual business, with both of us brokers and me a tax accountant, I no longer had to compete with other women in the workforce. Instead, my husband and I could now compete in the business community by providing our own quality services. With God's help we had exchanged that recession's adversity for opportunity. Our survival and success was humbling proof of what can happen when one refuses to give up. We'd come a long way.

Discovering ABWA

Discovering ABWA gave me a venue in which to further those old values I learned as a child and had carried me through so much and so far. I first learned about ABWA when I applied for one of the Four Townes Charter Chapter's annual scholarships. That was during my first semester at

UCF under the leadership of Dr. Covington. Money was still tight at that time and there were very few scholarships offered for "mature" students. Most were for the young kids graduating from high school. But I saw the little notice in the newspaper and decided to try. What a wonderful surprise to receive that $600 scholarship. It felt like much more; I felt so honored. Their scholarship enabled me to attend college that summer semester to continue on the fast track, full-time push I had set for myself. I was a woman in a hurry. I was still over 50 and getting more and more over 50 each year.

From the night of the award in May of 1995, these businesswomen continued to help me to grow and achieve my goals year after year. After the first graduation, I came back to join this wonderful, sometimes crazy group. They took me in and I became theirs. My ABWA sisters became my own personal cheerleaders and my support network. I soon discovered they, too, believed the belief my father taught me, that we can be whatever we want to be, if we just try. And that it's never, ever, too late to go back to school or go to college for the first time. We can get the education and credentials we need to accomplish our goals at any age or stage in life.

I have continued to be inspired, touched and challenged by the enthusiasm and just plain fun we've had and continue to have together. As I continued my quest for the kind of education that eventually qualified me to operate my own business, ABWA provided support for the journey that took me from office administration positions to co-ownership with my husband of a vibrant dual-service business.

Servant Leaders – Paying it Forward

I never forgot receiving my very first scholarship award in that roomful of smiling faces. All those professional women, of all ages, had a mission I was yet to discover. Three years later I had joined the Four Townes Charter Chapter simply because I was grateful for their help and was impressed with the support system for women. I wanted to give back something from the talents and abilities I'd been able to build on through higher education. This group was an important part of that process. They had been willing to invest in a 50-year-old woman's dream of getting a college education.

I discovered ABWA had a mission statement that completed my own belief system. Bringing together businesswomen from so many diverse occupations — and continuing to provide ways for us to grow personally and professionally through leadership, education, networking, support, and recognition — is an awesome mission! And the place where first I saw the power of this organization unleashed was when I attended my first Spring Conference. Women from all over the country — as far away as Hawaii — came together to share the ABWA mission.

I was finally able to attend a National Convention at Las Vegas, and it was an unforgettable experience. It is not easy to get away from accounting clients, but I scheduled time for another National when it was held in Richmond. I was not disappointed, and now I encourage new members to attend a Spring Conference or National Convention as early in their first years as possible.

How could I not serve on the committees and fundraisers? I was theirs. They owned me now. I simply wanted to give back to ABWA — not only the organization, but to individual women in our Four Townes area struggling to fulfill a dream or to gain a better chance in the workforce. Although I know networking plays a big part of growing our own businesses, that fact has not been my motivation. I had no thought of getting anything back for myself. Yet, I have received far more than I have given over these past few years.

I've brought guests to our meetings and watched their faces, as they comprehend the support and encouragement available with our members. Those who've joined have embraced the ABWA mission and benefited much. I do a tax seminar for our chapter each January and have been able to help members organize their business records better. I've gained new clients every year as a result of this small gift of time and sharing of knowledge gained from my education. It was a real joy to have chaired and served on the Education Committee. It was my chance to be on the giving end of the scholarship process.

My first brave step on the executive board was one term as Secretary. After that, how could I resist serving as Treasurer? Accounting was my "thing." I enjoyed two terms as Treasurer. Serving as co-chair of the first art auction we held was a mind-boggling experience. I wouldn't have known where to begin, but each member had talents that, when pooled together, created exciting success. We worked like crazy. But the thing we will always remember is the success and the fun!

I also had the pleasure of working with our Volusia Area Council and ABW Day Luncheon Celebration every September. Each chapter divided the workload plans and preparations. Our chapter supplied the *program* plans several times. I personally took on the task of securing a speaker and had the unique pleasure of meeting with local TV newscasters like NBC's Claire Metz and Fox News 35's Amy Kaufeldt. In person, these women were not much different from the rest of us. Their stories prove that women of any age can do anything they set their minds to if they are willing to work hard and obtain the tools needed to reach their goals. Claire Metz has remained a friend since those early programs.

Four Townes Charter Chapter's decision to elect me as their president for two years was a humbling, challenging and, yes, another fun experience. Then in 2005, what an honor it was to be chosen *Woman of the Year*. And the timing! It was the ultimate frosting on the cake for my first political campaign. What fun it was to list that award on my campaign platform.

Commissioner Janet Deyette

In 1995, my community voted to incorporate and became the City of Deltona. I began to develop an interest in being a part of the city's early planning, so in 1999 I volunteered as a charter member of our first Planning and Zoning Board. My real estate training, knowledge of zoning maps, and several terms on Realtor Grievance Committees, and the quasi-judicial Professional Standards Boards in Seminole and Volusia Counties had provided me with a perfect foundation for this position. I served for six years. Then from 2004 through 2005, I became interested in determining better ways to grow as a city and served on two Smart Growth environmental and development-redevelopment sub-committees.

By 2005, I had gained the confidence to start a major new chapter in my life. I would never have considered running for political office when I first met that ABWA group on scholarship award night. Back then I was uncomfortable speaking in public. I had no clue how to organize a campaign. But in 2005, I had the courage and the audacity to run for office for the first time in my life – at age 67 – and discovered all that experience and fun we'd had with the ABWA fundraisers was perfect training for political campaigning and fundraising. My husband was my very capable campaign manager. Our strategies all came together and I won by over 62 percent of the vote. I was elected to the Deltona City Commission, District 5, on November 8, 2005.

If I thought I was busy before, I was wrong. I'd had no clue what busy really could be. My life was no longer my own. The Commission public meetings are twice a month, each first and third Monday, with workshops scattered between. There is so much more to do. The Agenda package for main Commission meetings is generally two to three inches thick. That takes a few days to digest. My district citizens call me expecting their Commissioner to be able to solve all problems — and I do my best for them. City business is fast-paced, ever-changing and challenging. One has to keep up with everything, read everything, watch the news, and generally be ready for anything. Public life can be a battle or a consensus-building and rewarding experience all at the same time. I truly enjoy it. I know not to be sensitive, nor take things personally. I have learned what works best is to calmly examine every situation and respectfully explain the reasons for a particular opinion or decision. It is never boring, never predictable, and definitely worthwhile.

Top Ten Nomination!

Janet Clark, our Four Townes Chapter President, called me first thing in the morning of April 27, 2007. I was working on a tax return for one of the forty-some extensions we had filed on April 17th. I hadn't made it to our Executive Board meeting the night before because of a city-related meeting. "We decided last night at E-Board to nominate you for Top Ten," she cheerfully announced.

I was stunned. I was honored. But then she told me the rest. "You have until May 15 to prepare your story."

I had just finished what is always a grueling tax season and had looked forward to easing back a bit. I protested that I was tired and told her I probably wouldn't win anyway. "But we think you can. You're finished with the worst of the taxes. You can do it! You know all about ***you*** best!"

I quickly realized our members were not about to take no for an answer. They were certain I was going to win. So, I treated it like a college term paper and dug in, told my story, and finished just in time. Sometimes things got scary. There were constant interruptions. I don't think anyone realizes what an impossible task it is to condense one's life to a few sheets of paper when you've lived this long. There was so much to look up and verify. Once finished, my hectic life in the City of Deltona and the world of taxes and accounting resumed. I put Top Ten out of my mind, certain that I didn't stand a chance but satisfied that at least I hadn't let the group down. Each time we had a meeting they'd ask if I'd heard anything yet.

I was sitting at my computer catching up on emails and waiting for the rain to let up so I could head out to the Commission meeting when the call came. "Janet Deyette, this is Robin Necci from ABWA National headquarters," the voice said.

I answered, "Hi Robin," and then I stopped. "Wait a minute. Why are you calling me?"

She said I'd been chosen as one of the Top Ten Businesswomen. I think I screeched, "Oh my God!" a few times. Then, I said, "I need to buy a new suit. I need to register for National Conference right away. I need to make reservations. I have a City Commission meeting tonight. I was just about to leave the house. I'm not really going to care what they do tonight. Oh my God!"

What a delightfully crazy moment that was. Robin was laughing on the other end of the phone and telling me they'd told her she would enjoy giving the news.

And then I called my husband and Janet Clark — and I don't remember who else. I was hurrying. I needed to leave for the city meeting. I could barely think coherently. I could barely drive. I had broken my foot back in October 2006 and it had still not healed. I'd been in a cast until almost Christmas that year and it seemed to have healed. But in January, two metatarsal bones re-broke. Now I was wearing one of those clunky steel and foam and Velcro boots to keep the foot stabilized. I decided to buy a black suit with a long black skirt and a bright red blazer. I also bought a pair of tall black fashion boots. I figured the long skirt would hide the boot somewhat and the other fashion boot would even me up so my injury wouldn't be too noticeable. I was ready! Then the night we finished packing my other ankle cracked from overcompensating for the injured foot.

The next morning I decided to see if the new fashion boot would support my right ankle. It did. In a few hours, Mac and I were headed for Greensboro, North Carolina. I used a wheelchair at the airport and was able to get one at the hotel as well. Fortunately, I had thought to book a handicapped accessible room. As soon as the hotel staff discovered who we Top Tenners were, they treated us like royalty. ABWA members offered to give me a push whenever they saw me in the wheelchair. The other Top Tenners were wonderful helpers. Whenever we lined up, Tina Ackles and Rebecca Francis were on either side of me and held my elbows to boost me up each time we had to stand.

The excitement continued as we interviewed with the judges and received our Top Ten business cards and nameplate. We practiced our speeches under the very capable coaching of Laura Barron and delivered them at the Woman of the Year and Inner Circle Luncheon. My husband and several of our Four Townes members attended the conference. They were grinning proudly during the luncheon and during the onstage announcement and presentation of our trophies. We were introduced as the ABWA Top Ten American Businesswomen in the nation. What an unforgettable experience. What a humbling experience. Wow. This was a conference none of us would forget.

The judges had told us 2008 would be our year as ***Ambassadors*** for ABWA — and what a year it has been. My city did a press release to all the newspapers and television stations. People kept telling me, "I saw you in the paper. Congratulations!"

I dared to show off my trophy from the dais during commission comments at the end of the city meeting. Many of my constituents were delighted and have told me how proud they are to have me as *their* Commissioner. My clients tell me they are proud to have me as their accountant. Wow, again. I must keep my feet on the ground.

In the past I've often tried to describe ABWA's mission to friends and acquaintances and received limited responses. Now it seems to have become more real. We've gained a few more new members in our Chapter and others are expressing interest. I've had opportunities to speak and am looking forward to guiding and encouraging members in our chapter to consider accepting a nomination for next year's Top Ten event. I've been in two parades honored as the Top Ten Businesswoman for our Chapter.

District one's Spring Conference was held April 4th and 5th in Myrtle Beach, South Carolina. I dared to take off four days of our last few weeks' tax season to attend all sessions. Our Chapter President Janet Clark and Mary Lou Croteau and I took turns driving there. Three of us new Top Tens had an opportunity to give our speeches again during the luncheon — Rebecca Francis, Christine Wright, and I. I really didn't intend to attract any more attention, but ended up doing so because I fell right after the luncheon and slammed the back of my head on the tile floor. No one would let me get up. Betty Burns sat next to me with her bag of melting ice as we waited for an ambulance. Several people stood by asking if I was all right. I recognized Sue Huguenin, and my fellow Top Ten speakers, Rebecca and Christine. There I lay in my fine bright red blazer, my Top Ten badge and ribbon, my long black skirt with the matching black steel boot on the not yet healed left foot trying to assure the firemen that I knew who I was, where I was, and what day it was. I got to ride in a service elevator and on an ambulance. This was not my planned exit strategy.

The firemen kept me talking. They now know about ABWA and all that it means to be a Top Ten. We also talked politics and I told them I appreciated their assistance and that I love my city firemen. Rebecca and Christine followed us to the hospital and stayed until my release. Janet Clark and Mary Lou Croteau were there to take me back to the hotel. I had a tangerine size bump on the back of my head, but the CT scan proved that, while my foot was taking more than a year to heal, the hardest bones were in my head. That's a good thing. I had a concussion but would be okay after a few days' rest. For some reason, my fellow travelers, Janet and Mary Lou, would not allow me to take a turn on the drive back to Florida. Back home my husband vowed not let me travel again without him.

***

Preparing the information for this Top Ten award made me stop and take a fresh look at where life has taken me. I can see how not only the paths but also the dreams have gone through changes. As one of the survivors of the Hartford Circus Fire of July 6th 1944, I learned early not to take anything for granted throughout one's lifelong journey. From horse trainer, through motherhood and the thankfulness that comes of having three lively healthy boys, to small business owner wading through mountains of dog hair, to college student, to tax accountant, to city commissioner to Top Ten. This has truly been one awesome journey. The career changes that continued after turning 50 have proven to be more rewarding than winning the blue ribbons. It may not be as exciting and flashy as riding in a show ring, but it sure feels good to have the tools to meet a client's business and tax needs — and to have fun doing so.

I now receive a greater satisfaction from being able to help others. I now know that pain and loss, the sadness of divorce, the scary fear of losing material things can change us without destroying us. I've become stronger and more resilient. My dreams have changed. I still have goals. My husband and I would like to have our own building and are working toward that goal. But we've both learned to live more for today, to look for what can be done today more than always looking to the future. And, we make sure to carve out time just for each other.

Remember Dr. Covington, my Servant Leader? Because of what that man did for me in those critical first years of college, I now know how to be a Servant Leader. So now as a tax accountant, if I can focus on my clients' needs, if I can ease their fears of the IRS, remove their pain, preserve their dignity and solve their tax problems, then I can give them peace of mind and lead them to a better way.

As a City Commissioner, if I can focus on the needs of my citizens, listen to their concerns and their complaints, I can find solutions and be their voice at city hall.

In ABWA, if I can convince other women — especially those over age 50 — to reach for their dreams, to go back to school if that's what they want to do, or start their own business, I can show them the way. I've traveled the route. I know the path. I can share the excitement that infuses one's life when you step out and dare to follow your dream. If I can simply serve others . . . then I, too, can be a Servant Leader.

Rebecca Pulliam Francis

Most of my life I have been the one out of place. I was the tomboy who grew up on the farm where the world was mine to discover, the girl who played with bugs – ugh! - and played softball. I was the lone girl in the 4-H tractor maintenance project and one of the few women studying agriculture sciences. As one of the few women in a room of men at horticulture industry meetings, the novelty to me was the lack of other women interested in learning and working in the outdoor world, not that I was one of the few.

In motorsports, I could be found autocrossing — I even changed my own tires! — or teaching at competition driving schools and motorcycle safety foundation courses. One of my best friends in the horticulture industry, who has known me for 20 years, put my life into perspective. He said that physically I may be in a woman's body, but I think and act like a man. I do not operate as expected via stereotype; therefore, I intimidate men and women alike. My assertiveness and confidence, which would be considered assets for a man, are often seen as aggressiveness and arrogance in a woman.

My Career Path

My sense of confidence and work ethic were developed early. Raised on a 400-acre farm in the beautiful Knobs of Shelby County Kentucky with no brothers, I thought I could do anything. Work on the farm is day, night, day, and weekend work; we worked until the job was completed. I did not learn to work to the next break or quitting time. Through my first 4-H projects, tractor maintenance and swine, I also learned to finish the job by completing the paperwork and evaluating the project to make improvements for the next time. My mother was active in improving the state educational system at a time when the Kentucky schools were ranked 49th in the nation. As a child, I learned to shake the hands of strangers and ask for their support. In addition, I taught from the time I started school. When I came home from school, I set up a classroom and taught my little sisters what I had learned that day in school.

Admittedly, I liked competition and looked for challenges. Always of an inquiring mind, I threw myself into middle school and high school science fair projects on great circle routes, fermentation, and making atomics particles visible with dry ice. You should have seen my parents and me tracking down dry ice and active nuclear material. In today's world, we probably all would be arrested as potential terrorists!

And how I was able to conduct the fermentation project as a pre-teen even surprises me now. I visited distilleries in Louisville, and concocted some pretty nasty brews. I never really understood why anyone would want to taste my science experiment! Always up for a challenge, I exchanged summer visits with a French pen pal during my high school years. I signed up to take the college calculus final exam my high school calculus teacher arranged for our class to take at the university. And who but the senior class' Most Intellectual would announce her senior year that she was going to study nemotology (the study of microscopic worms) and plant pathology at college?

When I started my college studies at the University of Kentucky College of Agriculture, I learned the importance of network building. For the longest time, I was known as "Elizabeth Pulliam's daughter." My mother was recognized nationally for her lay leadership in cooperative extension. As a green freshman, I was able to walk into almost any administrative office at the Ag College and ask for information or help; but, I also had to develop my own identity. My field of study was Integrated Pest Management, which was an interdisciplinary program and took a holistic approach to plant health. My agriculture advisor thought I was crazy to continue to take math classes after the requirements were met. I thought the math classes kept my brain challenged.

One of my first paid jobs was working in the toxicology lab washing lab glassware with noxious chemicals and sacrificing lab rats. I found out very quickly that I needed to stay in the plant sciences. Plants do not whimper when you sacrifice them in the name of science. My other job was to scout 100-acre fields for crop pests and diseases. I realize now that the farmers were probably a little nervous about letting a teenaged girl wander around on their large farms by herself. Of course, I did not think anything of it.

At UK, I had another opportunity to travel abroad. In the early 1980s, about 20 of us invaded China as the first agriculture student exchange group to visit China after that country opened itself to visitors from the outside world. People we came in contact with were just as curious about us after a generation of isolation. Imagine a group of lanky teenagers dressed in jeans, boots, colorful shirts, and jewelry. To our Chinese hosts in their Maoist uniforms and with their conformist mindset, we must have looked and acted like aliens from another plant.

I once again learned that the world was very different outside of our country's boundaries. There were many restrictions: "Don't look in that or this direction" and "Do not point your cameras." Of course, the group had to sneak a peek at the soldiers with big guns standing guard at some facility or another.

There were also similarities. Some of the most gracious hostesses I have ever met invited us into their very humble homes. We also found that a number of our stereotypes about the Chinese were wrong and that pick-up basketball games were played around the world. The country school that we visited fielded a respectable above 6-foot team. And this compliment came from UK fans during a NCAA championship era.

As I graduated from the baccalaureate program, I discovered that the only jobs available to a fresh graduate in agriculture were to sell fertilizer and pesticides to white-haired farmers. Yeah, right. Even I knew that was not going to work well for a young woman! During college, I had also worked for the Kentucky Council for Burley Tobacco at trade shows. However, even the big tobacco companies were not interested in adding a young woman to their staffs that were almost exclusively male. I simply had to change my direction.

I went straight to work on a master's degree. As I was interviewing to continue my graduate studies, I ran across my first remembered overt discrimination. During the interview for one graduate program, the graduate coordinator flat out asked why I wanted to get a master's degree, and when I was going to get married and stay home to take care of babies. I told him I was not married and did not have plans to get married at the time. It surprised me then, but I am aghast now, that in the mid-1980s such a question was even thought to be asked or legally permitted. That was a portent of how the department was run. I found out that graduate students were really cheap labor and were kept on as lab technicians for as long as the graduate school allowed for their degree completion. By the 18-month point, I discovered I was not cut out to do labwork for someone else, day in and day out. Labwork was like farm work — days, nights, and weekends. Science was also like cooking — follow a recipe for concocting stains and fixants, check mycellial growth every four hours, etc. I must have produced thousands of histological slides when the process still used manual microtoming and fixing slides. With no mentoring and coaching for original scientific research, I challenged my advisor to get me through the thesis, and I completed the master's program after approximately two years.

My first full-time job was as a diagnostician in the Plant Disease and Insect Clinic at North Carolina State University, which was a return to extension work and helping producers by diagnosing and recommending legal solutions to plant health problems. The work was interesting and interacting with the producers, county agents, and university extension personnel was rewarding. Unfortunately, it reminded me again that being closed up inside four walls all day was not a preferred mode of life for me.

During this time, I also committed to the two long-term relationships in my life. I married my life partner in 1986.

Plus, in 1987, I found the American Business Women's Association through a fellow lab technician at the Plant Pathology Department at NCSU.

Through a connection made at an industry meeting, I was asked to join the largest wholesale nursery on the East coast as one of the few pest managers in the industry and as the first woman pest manager. I worked six years for the family who owned the nursery, until the owner sold the business to an international corporation. We grew the operation from less than 200 acres of containerized production and propagation greenhouses to about 400 acres, which included four sites in two counties and a large field-grown operation. I spent my days walking, scouting, and driving equipment around 400 acres. I gained more confidence in my problem solving abilities from repairing equipment and diagnosing plant health problems. I set up my own in-house research lab and trialed some of the first quick assays for virus detection and tissue culture in cooperation with research scientists. I also became the compliance and training coordinator to meet OSHA, EPA, NCDA, and Emergency Management requirements. Each day, I planned and supervised the spray crew. I encouraged my crew members to continue their education and pursue the pesticide license. During this time, I became involved with a number of the Green Industry organizations.

Several things came together to convince me that it was time for a change. When the business was sold to the corporation, I was working five and a half days per week and nine to ten hours per day. The new owners said that I deserved a huge raise —great! — plus, I was now expected to spend more time on the loading docks, even into the night, in addition to my regular schedule. I quickly realized that money is not everything. In addition, after a scare with a scratched cornea from dust and repeated bouts with respiratory problems from working with pesticides and fertilizers on a daily basis, I decided that I wanted to have a healthier life. And if my husband and I ever decided to have children that were healthy, I needed to change careers.

About this same time, I read an article on horticulture therapy, using horticulture and plants as a therapeutic mode. I soon discovered one of the most highly regarded programs in the state was located one mile from my house. The founding coordinator had been in the place for years. I thought that there probably was not a chance of her leaving. God works in mysterious ways. Very soon after that, the coordinator decided to go back to school and the position of director became available.

There is a story told about my interviews for the director position of the Greenhouse and Grounds Maintenance program. I met with a number of people, including the two instructors in the program. The story goes that as soon as I left the office after talking to them, they made a beeline to the dean's office and told him that they thought I was the one for the job, "Hire her. She has dirt under her fingernails; we know she will work." The dean and the president of the college told that story for years.

My nine years working in the local community at the local community college is the work of which I am most proud. I was able to use my horticulture skills and job experience to help build vocational and life skills for adults referred to the vocational program by the county mental health and social services agencies. My problem solving skills were applied to adapting work, tools, and curriculum to meet the needs of those adults. For some of these individuals, some up to 60 years old, these were the first real job skills that they had ever learned or practiced. Our program helped many individuals that society had "thrown away" become contributing citizens and productive workers in the community, sometimes for the first time in their lives.

In this role, I found my purpose for life and learned many of the skills of servant leadership and collaborative leadership. The Greenhouse Program gained international recognition, and I served as a consultant for starting similar programs nationally and internationally. In addition to serving as officer and president for the American Horticulture Therapy Association multi-state chapter, I became registered as a horticulture therapist by the national association at the Master level. I also learned the skills needed to coordinate regional and national conferences.

As the first woman horticulture department chair in North

Carolina community colleges, I also started the evening Horticulture Technology Program for working professionals. In order to build the new curriculum program in horticulture, we needed an outdoor space to serve as a classroom and lab. Two community members and I took the proposal to the college president to initiate the Arboretum to serve as the outdoor classroom for the Horticulture Technology program and expanded that vision to provide a facility to meet broader community horticulture needs. I spearheaded the development using a community-based programming model. I learned the challenges of coordinating the collaboration of diverse groups involved in the 30-member advisory committee, and state construction processes, as well as organizing major community fundraising efforts.

Working in the community in which I lived gave me the opportunity to be active in community organizations and activities. I was able to become very active in the committees at the college to include serving on the technology committee during a period when the college campuses took the step into the Information Age with campus-wide technology backbones for instructional delivery systems, a computer on every instructor's desk, and network access across the state. I also joined the college at the time the American Disabilities Act was signed. By nature of the vocational program, I became an active advocate for individuals with disabilities across the campus and in the community. In addition to the college's first disabilities and diversity committees, I worked with business and industry members through the Johnston County Disabilities Awareness Council, and served on the Johnston County Human Services Council. This was also a time my activity in ABWA kicked into high gear. As chapter president, I made a practice of delivering a bud vase to each new member at her place of business. Through my movement in the community, I was able to recruit a number of new members to ABWA.

Life is invigorating when you have a job you love and feel gives you purpose. At that time, I continually looked for new challenges. I changed my motorsport interest from autocrossing, in which I was twice the ladies' state champion in my class, to motorcycles. I was tired of looking at the back of my husband's helmet when we rode. Therefore, I took a Motorcycle Safety Foundation Beginning Riders Safety course. Of course, what better way to learn something than to teach it? I went to instructors' school as one of the first three women to teach MSF in North Carolina. That led to long, but invigorating, weekends of encouraging and coaching new riders.

Within three years of beginning teaching at Johnston Community College, the other instructors selected me as Teacher of the Year. With much help from my co-workers, I prepared the application package for the state Excellence in Teaching competition. I was selected as one of the top ten teachers in the North Carolina Community College system for 1995. The president and I attended the award ceremony together. As we were leaving, I naively asked him, "Where do I go from here?"

His response was, "You need your doctorate."

Before we returned to Smithfield that day, we stopped by the Adult and Community College Education department at North Carolina State University in Raleigh. I talked to the graduate program coordinator and came home with an enrollment packet in hand. In the spring of 1996, I took my first education class at NCSU. By that fall, I was accepted into the study program for the Doctorate of Education in Higher Education Administration. The classes that I took over the next six years were very beneficial to my understanding and practice of teaching adults, understanding community college policies, and organizational leadership.

With deadlines looming for completing my doctorate, I made the decision to give up my full-time job. As with any salaried position, the longer you are in the job, the more duties you pick up. My work had turned into day, night, and weekends again. I needed the time and clearer head to finish my course work and work on my dissertation research and writing.

While finishing my graduate degree, I was able to ply my talents and gain new experiences at several part-time positions. The first year, while I was finishing up classes, I held a graduate assistantship that gave me an opportunity to help plan an international research conference and produce a CD of the proceedings to include with the printed version, and supported courses that met via satellite broadcast to the other end of the state. The graduate assistant position gave me an opportunity to make contacts in the fields of adult education and the community college arena nationally and internationally.

I also was contacted by the Individualized Learning Center at Wake Technical Community College in Raleigh to serve as a part-time tutor of basic math skills for both the college developmental math courses and the GED test preparation program. I found that having worked in an industry that uses math, and teaching math throughout the horticulture classes, I was able to bring a practical application approach to teaching math that many times gets lost in a classroom setting. The position at Wake Tech kept me in contact with the day-to-day operations of a community college. As I drew to completion of my dissertation, the Individualized Learning Center at Wake Tech hired me to a full-time position, and that is where I am currently employed.

During the time that I was conducting my research and completing the onerous task of writing my dissertation, I put many community activities and relationships on hold. Always looking for the challenge, I took upon myself the task to conduct and write qualitative research, this from a purely quantitatively trained, scientific mind. I did discover that as a systems thinker, the newer scientific thinking of quantum mechanics and complexity theory has broad reaching merit in bringing quantitative and qualitative sciences together. I actively seek out challenges, and this one made me work to achieve a goal harder than I have ever worked before in my life. At this point, I see the diploma as a survival certificate.

My ABWA Experience

I have been a member of the Johnston Charter Chapter, as well as a national member of ABWA, for the past 20 years. My ABWA sisters have supported and encouraged me. They have supported me through my husband's deployment in Desert Storm, through job and career changes, through my application and receipt of the national ABWA president's scholarship in 2003, during the times I had to back off a little on taking on major leadership positions in the chapter, and during the writing process for my dissertation. A number of my chapter members helped me with transcription and the editing of my dissertation. My chapter members kept telling me that they knew I would be selected as a Top Ten for ABWA when I completed the doctorate. They have been the most enthusiastic about my receiving this recognition.

In addition, I have watched the individual chapter members grow over the 20 years. Of the 14 members I have sponsored into ABWA, almost everyone has served as a chapter officer, many as president. I have watched the younger members, who in the beginning were barely able to stand up at their seats and introduce themselves, become president of the chapter and conduct meetings. I have watched the members who started as career secretaries gain the confidence, as well as the skills, to go for positions with more responsibility and/or gain the confidence to start their own businesses. I have seen the mothers, who felt that they had to do everything for their families, learn to let go and allow them to learn to become responsible adults. I have also seen members who have never gotten farther away from home than they can drive find the enjoyment of getting away overnight and taking the first airplane flight. I have seen members who have gone through major family and medical crises call on the support and encouragement of the chapter members.

As I said in my speech at the 2007 National Women's Leadership Conference, over my life I have had many cheerleaders, a number of patrons and sponsors, and a few role models. One role model, Bonnie Hooks, is one of my Johnston Charter Chapter sisters. She has been a member for 27 years. When I joined 20 years ago, she was one of the members I looked to to answer questions. In my eyes, she is a prime example of a servant leader and a quintessential southern lady. Although she has had a corporate career involving cutbacks, company sales, and reorganizations, Bonnie always comes out with grace and class. Bonnie is quick to help in family and friend emergencies. As a chapter member, she is one of the first to volunteer for committee work or chapter projects.

Bonnie is also one of the loudest voices to encourage and cheer me on in my endeavors and achievements. I have followed Bonnie's example in taking on leadership roles in the chapter through the years. As soon as I graduated in December 2006, members of my chapter encouraged me to run for 2007-2008 chapter president.

I have also gained many friends across the country from regularly attending ABWA spring conferences and national conventions. We recognize each other from past meetings and continue to build those connections. The local and national members of ABWA have encouraged me to grow and bloom from a lab technician who was, as Bonnie puts it, "a little rough around the edges" to a confident woman who is nationally and locally recognized as a leader in her profession and as a professional business woman.

Pay Forward

I will continue to serve as a coach and mentor to numerous women starting careers and continuing established careers. As an educator, I always recommend that a woman entering the workforce for the first time, or a woman retooling her skills to change careers, find a professional networking group that provides networking support and continuing educational opportunities.

I recently had a radio interviewer ask me if I thought

there is still a need for national broad-based organizations, many of which started after World War II when women were first entering the workforce in large numbers. My answer to him was having a broader professional network is extremely beneficial when employees change careers as many as six to seven times in a working life and jobs as many as 20 times during their working life. The profession-based networks can usually only help a person get the next position in the same field. Networking organizations that cross many professions provide the contacts to take that very scary step of changing careers. ABWA is one of the premier professional organizations that provides that networking support and educational opportunities across a broad and diverse range of professions.

Epilogue

This year has been a year of awesome privilege: a year of honor, change, and chaos management.

As previously stated, my chapter elected me to serve as the 2007-2008 chapter president. They commissioned me to make changes that would turn our chapter around for members and the community. Taking that mandate, I led our chapter to change paradigms and projects. We changed our fundraising project from a walk-a-thon held for many years in the fall to a women-in-business networking exposition held in the spring, which turned out to be very successful. In addition, we changed our awards banquet from April to June with great results.

During the year, my chapter recognized me in celebration of my twentieth year as an ABWA national and Johnston Charter chapter member. At the end of the year, I was named Chapter Woman of the Year. To me, it has tremendous meaning when close friends who know you warts and all wish to honor you with this award. Then I was asked to serve as chapter president for a second term to continue the progress that we have made. This is unprecedented in the 29 years our chapter has been in existence.

I also had the privilege of attending two district conferences. The three newest chapter members and I made a road trip to the District I conference at Myrtle Beach. They caught the enthusiasm and all three will be serving as officers for the 2008-2009 chapter year. They know that I need at least one keeper, because I disappeared during the Myrtle Beach conference. I ended up going to the emergency room with a fellow Top Ten who tried to crack her head open on the slate floor at the motel. I do not usually carry my cell phone to the seminars, so of course when we had to leave I had no way of contacting my group to let them know where I had gone or to contact them to let them know when I would be back. Ah, the stories we can tell about ABWA spring conferences — but won't.

I also attended the District 4 conference in Niagara Falls. This trip I traveled with a long-time chapter member and friend. We have attended numerous conference and conventions together, so we had a great slumber party. We allowed enough time to play tourists. At this conference, our chapter received the newsletter award, for the first time in our chapter history. Yahoo! They heard us all the way back in North Carolina.

During this busy year, another area in which I have dealt with chaos management is with my family. Shortly after the 2007 ABWA convention, my sister who runs a cattle farm and is caretaker to our mother, broke her back in a rollover automobile accident. My blessed husband followed the call for him to temporarily move to help take care of my family and farm duties in order for me to maintain my fulltime employment status in North Carolina. I have been the long-distance family counselor by phone and made monthly trips back to Kentucky, thanks to the consideration of my supervisor and family medical leave policies.

As of this writing, I have accepted a position to teach 6th and 7th grade math and science to students who did not pass end-of-grade tests. I have spent six years working with adults and teens who realized the importance of education and returned to complete the GED. Almost all have told me that their paths to dropping out of high school started in middle school. This is my opportunity to help break the dropout cycle, for at least a few students.

This year I also started a home-based business as an independent wellness consultant with a business partner and fellow ABWA member who I met at the national convention in September. Teachers do not teach for the money; therefore having the additional income will allow me to fulfill my life purpose of teaching and encouraging life-long learning, and to fulfill my passion of helping people live healthier, more balanced lives.

Christina Robinson Grochett

I recall that it was a cool March morning when my father told me that "home is where you hang your hat." At the time, I did not realize the impact those seven words would have on my life. Even more, I was unaware of the way they would shape my vision of life.

Growing up in a military family, my perception of normalcy was skewed. My father would regularly come home and tell my mother "Pack our bags; we are moving."

This was a standard practice. While routine for those in the military, my parents did not know that each of these moves and changes would lead me on a journey of vast experiences and create inside me a hunger for constant change.

When thinking of change and how change guides our lives, it is important to for me to remember that in the first eighteen years of my life, I moved seventeen times. Each time, I was presented with a new experience, a new culture and uniquely different surroundings. These changes would ultimately shape my perception of the world. This chapter is a look at how this life and journey has transformed Christina Robinson Grochett into the person I am today and how this journey will help shape the world of tomorrow.

There are two extremely vivid times in my life where I believe the path I was on was drastically changed. The most memorable time was at ten years old. My mother was a very dedicated stay at home mother. She taught me much of what I know. We had recently transferred to a new home in Texas. Just like any mother, she wanted me to have it all. Knowing that I had a love for music, she did everything in her power to help me realize that dream. She also drove me from house to house to sell Girl Scout cookies when I was a Brownie, volunteered as my troop leader, and took me to dance and gymnastics lessons. A self-taught seamstress, my mother would stay up sewing costumes for children in my classes to pay for my piano and singing lessons.

She taught me a unique art of bartering. For years she would clothe our performance groups in beautiful costumes and I would get music training. Those singing lessons paid off and at eleven years old I was making children's records with Silver-Burdett Record Co.

That year, I began spending many hours in the recording studio. Mickey Gillie's Recording Studio, of *Urban Cowboy* fame, became my weekend home. Making children's records was so much fun and it was my first paying job.

My mother made me save every check and those checks ultimately paid for my freshman year of college. After six months with Silver Burdett, my father came home with that look on his face. "We are moving to Baton Rouge, Louisiana," he said. "I am sure you can sing there."

The path I thought I was on immediately changed that day. Three weeks later, I was in Baton Rouge.

Louisiana is a great place to live. However, unlike Texas which holds a largely transient population, most Louisianans are lifelong residents. Out of all the places I have lived, Louisiana was the hardest to adjust to. However, after awhile, those Cajuns do warm up and they truly have the best food. I had the great fortune to spend a few years there and join an amazing performing group. I attended a performing arts high school and had the opportunity to travel all over. As an All State Choir second soprano, I was one of several selected to perform at Carnegie Hall and go to Vienna.

Once again it seemed like all was back in play. I assumed I would go to LSU and major in vocal performance. I even believed I would graduate and go to New York. I wanted to make it to the top. However, in my junior year of high school, my father was transferred again. I remember my eyes welling with tears as I left the school and friends I loved. I would never return to music again. Although I love music with the deepest of passions, I do believe some part of me was left in Louisiana the day we moved away.

It became time to apply for college. I had thought about majoring in music or making the dreamed about move to New York City. I remember my father telling me that I could always do music after college, but a business degree would get me where I needed to go. That day I made the decision to go to Texas A&M University. This university was a fantastic experience for me; however, music was not on the list. However, the Agricultural and Mechanical University would change my views on the world and drive me to desire success. Throughout college, I worked as everything from a door to door salesperson to managing the 12th Man Foundations Alumni drives. All of this provided me with great experiences.

I also completed a two summer internships with Ferguson Enterprises, a large plumbing distributor. I would never have dreamed I would be driving a forklift and selling toilets at twenty. However, upon graduation, I accepted a position with Ferguson in their management trainee program. This position truly changed my vision of hard work. My first three months I spent at the receiving and loading dock. Anything you can imagine for your kitchen, bathroom or sewer, came through this dock and our shipping manager. I was at work for 6:30 a.m. shipments and finally out the door at 7:00 p.m. After awhile, I was allowed to move inside. I had the pleasure of moving into the kitchen and bath gallery. This was when I realized that I had creativity and an innate ability to innovate. I worked with customers to help them attain the kitchens and baths they could only dream about. After about six months, I moved to Houston and became a showroom consultant. I worked with all of the top designers in Houston and provided fixtures for many of the famous Houston elite such as Hakeem Olajuwon.

It was a fantastic first job and I learned how to deal with people of all levels. However, I eventually felt the need for a change. Through my dealings in the showroom, I met a CEO of a healthcare company. He offered me an opportunity to go into medical device sales. Most significantly, I was given the chance to ultimately become their Director of Marketing.

I had an opportunity to assist our company through the IPO process as well as a few acquisitions. This was a thrilling time. However, the healthcare industry at the time was facing some major challenges due to federal changes. In two years, the stock plummeted and I found myself looking for a new position.

One of my old Ferguson friends was now in the staffing industry and thought I would make a great fit. I went to work for Robert Half International and spent a number of years in the staffing industry. It was a fabulous time; the tech market was booming and jobs were plentiful.

I thrived on the opportunity to give people the gift of jobs. It was during this time that I became involved with the American Business Women's Association (ABWA) and the Houston Area Professional Express Network. The ladies in this organization helped me get my staffing business off the ground. They empowered me to believe that anything was possible and I could do anything I set my mind to. I held numerous officer positions as well as serving as President of the Houston Area Council. However, when 9/11 hit, the whole industry fell. During 9/11, I was placing financial staff. The Big 6 accounting firms became the Big 4 and Enron fell. Enron, who was one of my major clients, went under and I was struggling to obtain new clients due to the market downfall.

I made the decision once again to find a new career. The questions that weighed on my mind were how, and where?

Then ABWA came along again. It was a Saturday morning and I had been invited to an American Business Women's Education event. I thought this would be a great learning opportunity. University of Phoenix was represented at this event and as I spoke to the representative, she asked me if I had ever thought of getting a Masters degree. I mentioned to her I was at a fork in the road. Although I was still in the staffing industry, I knew I needed a career change. She then asked if I would be interested in working for the University of Phoenix. Knowing very little, I said sure and gave her my name. A few days later, her boss called and suddenly I was going to get an interview. After numerous meetings, I was offered a position to be a corporate relations specialist. I could help University of Phoenix become a household name in the Houston market. I accepted.

Every now and then we are able to experience something amazing. When I began my career at the University of Phoenix Houston Campus, I had this opportunity. I remember my first day of employment very well. At this time the campus had only one location and approximately 35 employees. A little more than a year later, we were told to more than double our staff and open two additional locations. Little did I know that I had embarked on what would become a remarkable journey and time of creativity and tremendous growth.

In 2005, I took on the role of Director of Enrollment. It seemed as if every day, we were creating some new process, trying some new method that might have seemed to many of us as being sheer daily madness. However, living in a culture of change and innovation bonded everyone together and has created some tremendous relationships. At the end of the day, it was all about supporting and graduating our students. For the first time, I was working for something I truly believed in, educating those that want to be successful and developing community leaders.

I was given an opportunity to build the third largest campus in the university. I thought to myself, "How do you double your staff in three months, change the way business is done, and still be profitable?"

While that year seems like a blur, it was truly a learning experience. We managed to more than double our staff, add over 20 new programs to our offerings, triple our management team and completely change how we deliver service to our students. I recall Brian Mueller, our new CEO, had just stepped in and told each of us that our focus was all about our students and delivering a quality program. With this in mind, everything we did was in the best interest of the student. Our service level and students were most important and our job was to help our students be successful. Every staff member knew that at the end of the day, our students were our priority, and our jobs were to help them graduate. We were to be mentors to our students, our staff, and our faculty.

This vision and culture change transformed my campus. We became leaders. We lived every day with the passion to know we could drastically impact someone's life. A year later, I had another opportunity to take over as Campus Director for the Houston Campuses. The most important time in this scenario is graduation.

I remember scenes from my first graduation as the Campus Director. I was in Toyota Center, where the Houston Rockets often play. More than 15, 000 students, parents, children and staff were in the stadium. I had the privilege to shake every single graduate's hand and hand them all their degrees. I saw the smiles, the tears, and the unwavering excitement in the eyes of each and every one of them. This was a very different experience from my own graduation at Texas A&M University. It was an exciting time for these students, and for many of them we were their last chance. Their children were watching them graduate instead of their parents watching them. Many of the graduates were the first in their families to obtain a degree. For these students, their degrees will change their lives and the paths they have been on forever.

Over the last 15 years, I have seen many companies succeed and fail. I have worked for many of them. As CEO for one of the most successful campuses in our history, I have seen three significant drivers of success. These drivers have assisted me in creating an amazing environement for growth and change. First, hire the best people and surround yourself with those who are better than you. They will allow you to be creative and keep you from any sense of complacency. You might have great ideas, but implementing them is a completely different process. Identify your weaknesses and build a team around them.

Second, ensure you never fear change. I recall a quote from Margaret Engelbreit, "If you don't like something change it; if you can't change it, change the way you think about it." I consistently tell my staff to never get to comfortable in their cube. As a new Director, I began to move my staff regularly. At first they thought this was strange. Now they are comfortable with it. This regular change allows them to embrace other individuals and learn new methods. When you have sat next to the same person for 5 years, what new things will you learn? More importantly it drives home to the staff that change is a good thing when done correctly. My directors know always to provide two solutions for change. It is all a mindset. This mindset creates opportunity.

Third, take risks, Be willing and open to accepting all ideas. Even if the ideas sound crazy, sometimes those can be the most effective and grant the biggest impact to the organization. Lastly and most importantly, remember your people are the most integral part of the process. When all the profits are stripped away, the furniture moved and the doors close, the people not the business made you a success.

Julie Kangas D.D.S.

My selection as a Top Ten businesswoman has been an amazing experience. I never expected to be acknowledged or singled out for what I do — living my life and trying to be the best I can be in my career. What a wonderful opportunity this is!

I still find it surprising to think of myself as a Top Ten businesswoman. To me, my business skills have always seemed separate and secondary to my professional skills as a practicing dentist. I have been a dentist for over 25 years and I own a practice with my husband. Together we lead a team of healthcare professionals who dedicate ourselves to enhancing the lives and health of our family of patients. We believe we are unique in our community and we do take pride in this.

Becoming a dentist was not my first idea of what I'd be when I grew up. Like many of my Top Ten colleagues, my plans have changed a few times, but I believe dentistry is a good match for my interests, personality, and skills. My earliest recollection of what I wanted to be was a nurse. From an early age, I realized I liked helping people feel better — physically and mentally. My second career plan, which I was quite passionate about, was to be a writer. I loved writing every time I had a chance, and I acquired some experience writing for my school newspaper, and later became an editor. While in high school, about the time I started dreaming of a career with a major magazine, I discovered chemistry and my plans changed again.

I thought chemistry was fascinating, and I had a young teacher who really grabbed my interest. In spite of the fact that so many of my classmates complained about hating chemistry, I was hooked! I decided I wanted to study and work in a field that related to science. I was instinctively drawn to healthcare rather than research or a more technical field such as engineering. After rejecting nursing and pharmacy, I started to think about dentistry. I liked the idea that it wouldn't involve 24 hour hospital shifts or the life and death decisions of medicine, but would offer the advantages of working directly with patients and impacting their health in a meaningful way. Selecting a career with interesting work and good income opportunities seemed like a smart idea. Both of my parents grew up during the Great Depression, and my mother was effective in instilling the values of hard work and being responsible for myself. I lost my father to cancer soon after I began high school, but Mom believed in education and gave me the encouragement I needed to pursue my dreams.

I never considered that going into the dental profession would be more of a challenge because I was a woman. My high school guidance counselor tried to talk me out of taking "all that science" and thought I was crazy not to stick with English as a college major. But she did support me in being able to study and become whatever I wanted to be. My immediate goal was to go away to college out of state, but my family encouraged me to attend college locally, and save the money I would need for graduate school. My desire to stay home among friends and the incentive of getting my own car for graduation helped me decide to attend Boise State University, located just a few miles from my home.

My savvy mother and a special college placement exam allowed me to jump into college with sophomore standing. My mother, who did not attend college, figured out the curriculum well enough to get me into general chemistry during the summer after high school graduation. I was apparently one of the first persons to skip first semester chemistry, which I accomplished by way of my two years of high school chemistry. My plan was an "outside the box" idea for the chemistry department at that time, and they did not even have a placement exam. With department head approval, I received full course credit by successfully passing the summer school course. Bypassing some of the usual freshman year classes allowed me to enter both advanced biology and organic chemistry in the fall. It looked like a reasonable schedule to me, but I had no idea how rigorous the academic challenge would be. I rose to the occasion and had a successful first year, but felt almost over my head in chemistry and science classes with older upper classmen. I soon decided to take advantage of BSU's degree program in pre-dental studies, with a biology emphasis, which allowed me to take the courses needed for dental school and not be bogged down by classes which were not needed for professional school. By taking just one additional summer school class the next year, I was able to complete my degree requirements and graduate in three years. My letter of recommendation was drafted by a pre-dental committee which included the pre-dental advisor and three other professors which I was able to request. I believe their support helped me a great deal, because I happily accepted an offer to attend the USC School of Dentistry for next fall's incoming class.

During my years at BSU, I enjoyed studying French, beginning German, and several economics classes. I participated in a pre-dental internship program which required observation and reporting on visits to several dental offices. I had summer jobs in retail and a brief time hostessing at an upscale steakhouse. I also joined a sorority, and served in most officer positions including chapter president. As president, I was required to live at the chapter house even though I commuted from my home just a few miles away. Living at the house was a terrific opportunity to get closer to other women very different from the close friends I clung to from high school. We had fun nights of popcorn and movies, "exchange" events with the fraternities and several formal dances and dinners to which we invited our boyfriends or dates. I was able to get a taste of the national organization by attending an annual national convention in Seattle, and an area leadership program in Vancouver BC, Canada.

While involved in my sorority, my favorite positions were as rush chairman and pledge advisor. I loved the enthusiasm of new members who were hungry to learn and contribute to our chapter. We were a fun-loving group of women with diverse personalities and goals who were passionate about our bonds of sisterhood. As rush chairman, I was able to plan the activities for rush week in order to draw as many potential members into our chapter as possible. I chose themes for each of the three nights of rush week and planned our decorations, costumes and member roles, much like putting on a play with a different script each night. My crowning glory was pledge night, for which I orchestrated a candlelight ceremony for each of our invited guests, during which we held hands in a circle and sang our most emotional official song. I felt I had achieved my goal when the event ended with all our members and most of the rushees in tears and hugging each other. I believed I discovered that night that emotion sells better that anything else we could offer! That year was the most successful rush we had in many years; more were pledged to our sorority than all of our competitors. As pledge advisor, it was my role to mentor and teach these young college students about the sorority and ensure that they upheld our standards of membership. These happy memories of sisterhood remained with me throughout my life, and sustained me through some lonely times at graduate school. Many of my sorority experiences were also very similar to the great times I later enjoyed in ABWA.

Moving to Los Angeles alone as a twenty-one year old female from Idaho was a huge adjustment— even more than the intense competitive environment of professional school. I recall picking up a list of apartments for the neighborhoods near the campus, which gave me no information on which areas would be safer for a single, naive female. USC was bordered by tough neighborhoods on three sides, and I believe I was very fortunate not to have moved into this area. Since I never found a manager on the premises at most of these apartments, the first apartment that I found available was a studio in the Wilshire area of Los Angeles, about a 15 minute drive from school. I lived in a small apartment building managed by a kindly elderly lady who befriended me and helped me feel welcome. My sister and her family lived about 50 miles away from school near Disneyland, and I spent many weekends with her to help escape my homesickness.

The first semester of school was grueling, and I was often frustrated by the endlessly long lectures, the intense competition and the hours and number of classes. I realized however, that most of my classmates were in the same boat as I was, so I volunteered to serve as freshman class president with another student in order to get to know the other students quickly. I also joined a dental fraternity after I was assured that they welcomed women students, as long as I didn't expect preferential treatment! My dental fraternity is also where I met and began dating my husband. A year ahead of me in dental school, Randy gave me a lot of valuable advice and assistance on many lab projects. We dated for three years until he graduated, and were engaged just before my senior year.

Women were definitely in the minority in my dental school class; we numbered just 12 out of 120 freshmen. Many of the other dental schools had begun to approach equality within the incoming classes, but USC's 100 year history wasn't in the forefront of change. I didn't see it as a big problem; in fact it was sometimes an advantage in that the instructors learned our names a little more quickly. Most of our instructors were friendly and willing to help all the students equally, but a few were reportedly harder on the women students. I didn't experience this personally until my third year, when we began to practice mock state board exams on patients. A powerful alumni dentist had returned to the school to work with students after several years' absence, and he participated in grading many of my cases. I was steadily improving and passing all the procedures, so I was shocked to be called in to the department head's office at the end of a trimester grading period. He informed me that I was on academic probation due to a failing grade in a clinic! I'm sure I broke down in tears in his office, but I protested immediately, that I knew I had clearly passed every test. When he showed me my grade record, I couldn't believe that several entries were below passing. It was clearly obvious to me that several penciled in grades had been altered; the grades had actually been lowered after they had been shown to me! I know the instructor was in a tough spot; he seemed to believe me and sympathize with my position, but to call the senior dentist on his falsified report could mean losing his job. I had not been aware of his bias against women, but later discovered that he felt women didn't belong in the dental profession! Without admitting any injustice towards me, the department chair said that he would arrange a way for me to make up the projects in time to erase the failing grade from my record. Over the next several weeks I spent extra time doing additional cases with a calm and compassionate dentist who volunteered his time with students. The skills I gained from him compensated somewhat for the bruise to my ego, and I knew I had gained his respect when I later received some referrals of his patients who had moved to my area after graduation.

I graduated on schedule in June 1981, as one of the three youngest in the class. I had passed both sections of the written national boards during the previous year, and my California clinical boards were completed in April, two months before graduation. Three weeks after my state boards, Randy and I were married and we were able to take a wonderful honeymoon in Europe. At that time, the six week time delay waiting for board results was "dead time" for dental students: no license and no degree until graduation day meant no work opportunities! After enjoying this free time for my wedding and honeymoon, I was then ready to begin my career, and couldn't wait to start my first job.

I moved to Escondido, and realized I would have to look in San Diego for a position with a dental clinic or private office. I found my first job from a newspaper ad, and was hired as the first woman dentist at a clinic which employed five other associate dentists. The staff told me they had convinced their boss that it was time they had a woman dentist on the staff. I worked there about a year before I was ready to try something different, with a better salary and chances to expand my skills. Even in the short time I was in that office, I built a following of patients who thought I was "more gentle" than the dentists they had seen in the past. I worked in several different offices over the next few years, including a clinic for low income patients in Escondido. I didn't find my employers were unfair to me as a woman; in fact, many dentists interviewed me because I was female, and thought I might draw more woman patients and families to their offices.

The only time I was ever fired was from my second job, where my husband also worked on different days of the week. He called me one night as he was driving home from work to tell me that we had both been let go. My response was, "What? They can't fire me without even telling me in person!"

At my next (and last) day of work, I demanded to speak

to the clinic manager. I told him they couldn't fire me by just telling my husband. His answer was, "We thought he had bigger shoulders and would be able to handle it better." I had heard rumors that their office was struggling financially, but eventually learned that the practice was going bankrupt and the owners had failed to pay many of the suppliers who had equipped their extravagant facility. Overall, that office provided several very good learning experiences!

I soon began to see some patients in the small office my husband had opened in Escondido. Our space was not large enough for both of us together, but we alternated days as we both worked in different locations to supplement our schedules. Five years after graduation, we leased a large space in a new shopping center, and designed and built an office that would accommodate both of us as partners as well as other dentists and staff.

One of my greatest opportunities in my early years in practice came when someone invited me to join a Leads Club that was starting in Escondido. There were 10 to 15 women business owners in our group and our objective was to help each other build our businesses by referral. We were only allowed one type of business in each category, so I not only acquired many of these women as clients, but also learned a lot by hearing stories about how each person operated her business. As one of the youngest members, I don't think I reciprocated well in the referral category, but I was enthusiastic and gained a lot from their experiences.

We stayed together for several years, and I made many lifelong friends in the group. Eventually we stopped having our regular meetings because we were not expanding our group and many of us were well along in our business careers. We still continued to get together on occasions such as business open houses, and social events. This was my first experience with a businesswomen's networking group, and it was completely positive. I developed a great respect for women in business, and found them to be good communicators, goal oriented, and wonderful mentors.

I also started attending meetings with a new group of women dentists who were forming in San Diego. We scheduled speakers to gain education hours and shared insights on our practices as well. I did not have mentors in the dental field at this time, but practicing with my husband was an advantage. We discussed most of the office issues we had to face, and because we had both worked in several different offices in our early years of practice, we had the opportunity to deal with a variety of situations with our patients. We had our ups and downs with employees too, and hired consultants twice to help us sort out the conflicts and unclear expectations that continued to crop up. In hindsight I now see that we were too lenient, and we frequently had some staff who would take advantage of our lax attitudes about management. We were too naïve to realize that allowing some staff members to run over our policies actually created resentment among the hard-working ones. We liked maintaining a fun office environment and usually sponsored two parties a year, a Christmas party at one of our staff member's homes, and a summer party to which we invited staff to bring their children. We celebrated Halloween by dressing in costume at our office and taking the entire staff to lunch. We also did some travel together; one summer we took all the office staff and spouses to Yosemite for a long weekend. We camped in the tent cabins, had team building meetings and campfires, and rewarded everyone with dinner at the elegant Ahwahnee Hotel.

We had many team members come and go, but were also successful in keeping some loyal staff for many years. We loved having new patients come to the office and finding out they often had connections with our team members who had grown up locally. In California, a transient population is the norm, even among our patients and our staff, so we have always been proud of our long term employees. One of the greatest factors in our success has been the number of staff who have been with our office over 10 years, and several for more than 20. We make an event out of anniversaries: for each year of employment we send flowers commemorating the number of years they have worked in our office. Every five years we give special gifts, an office watch or vacation bonus, and an after work party for all the staff to celebrate the honoree's milestone. As our staff grew, so did our practice, and eventually an opportunity arose for us to purchase land and build our own dental building.

The land that we found was just a few blocks down the street from our current office. We loved the location, and the greatest benefit was that it was even closer to a major freeway. We had actually been watching and asking about the site for quite a while, but had heard only that the owner lived out of the area. When the "for sale" sign went up on the site, my husband excitedly called to inquire that same day. After reaching the listing agent, we couldn't believe that an offer had already been accepted! Within a few days, we received a call from a physician in the medical group in our center, inviting us to join them in building a professional office complex. Apparently they knew the real estate agent personally and were called even before the signage appeared on the property. We were a little disappointed, but still liked the location well enough to believe that a share of the property was better than none at all. Over the next several years, the delays with annexing to the city and the fear of foreclosure by the landlord caused our physician partners to back out of the project. A long seven years later, our perseverance paid off and we moved into our dream dental office. We had beautiful, timeless Spanish architecture, spacious and comfortable offices and treatment rooms, and a mortgage payment to cause heart failure! We certainly had our growing pains once again, but have never regretted the decision, and hope never to move our office again.

Several years after starting our practice, my husband and I attended a dental meeting that had a profound influence on our professional and personal lives. A little known organization in dentistry, The American Academy of Dental

Practice Administration, is dedicated to building practice management skills and assisting dentists in balancing work and personal life. We were in awe just associating with many of the dentists and consultants in the group. We discovered that many of the speakers we heard at dental meetings were members, and they were willing to share their success with other dentists like us. We decided that we would like very much to apply for membership. We understood that there were criteria for selection, and after finding dentists who would sponsor us, we believed we were ready. We were separately interviewed by a committee at the annual meeting, but were both advised the next day that we had not been accepted. I was humiliated, and concluded that I should probably just drop the idea of membership and continue attending as a guest. My husband, who had always been more persistent than I, was not so ready to give up.

Fortunately, our sponsor dentist intervened on our behalf, and soon contacted us about building our resumes to make us stronger candidates. I was lacking in leadership experience, so that year I ran for and was elected president of the San Diego Women Dentists. I also developed and presented a speaking program to the senior dental students at USC about dental practice management, and how to be a good employee dentist. Two years later, we applied for membership again, and were installed as the first husband and wife dentists of the Academy of Dental Practice Administration.

Last year, as I prepared my speech for the ABWA Top Ten luncheon in Greensboro, we were asked to describe an experience with a Servant Leader who had significantly impacted our life. Recalling my academy sponsor's support, I realized how he had helped me turn an obstacle (my rejected application for membership) into a stepping stone. Through his guidance, I gained leadership as well as speaking experience, and was ultimately rewarded with my coveted academy membership. During my active years building a dental practice and a family, I had failed to realize that I had become complacent about my professional growth. My Servant Leader refocused my attention, and gave me the push that got me back on track. I am forever grateful for the mentorship and support he gave me that forever changed my future direction.

I discovered ABWA just over 10 years ago, after reading about a new businesswomen's group forming in my community. I attended an open house meeting, and was soon signed on as a charter member of the Soaring Eagles chapter of the American Business Women's Association. I was ready to get involved in a networking group again, and found I was quickly immersed in meeting women from diverse occupations. Not all of our members were business owners, but all were take charge individuals who accepted the challenge of creating their own career success. I enjoyed the speakers, and was inspired by the energy of the first officers of our chapter, who talked about ABWA to everyone they met, and always had membership applications in their cars. I sat on the sidelines the first few years, but I did sponsor several of my staff for membership and encouraged women I met to attend our monthly chapter meetings. I attended regularly, and was active in most of our fundraisers. However, I declined to run for an office even though I was encouraged many times. One dear long time member, Kate, who had transferred from another chapter to the north, would frequently whisper in my ear, "If you'd take an officer position, you'd be a good candidate for Top Ten!"

Eventually, I accepted a position as Program Committee chair, and then was elected VP of Membership. The best thing I learned about being on the leadership team was that this was where the real fun happened!

At my first national conference in Grapevine, Texas, I had a great time getting to know my fellow chapter members better while learning more about the national scale of ABWA. The politicking that went on in the hallways between the meetings was unbelievable, and I was impressed by the campaigners who dressed in color coordinated outfits to catch our attention on behalf of the candidates for national office. I learned the meaning behind the phrase, "everything's bigger in Texas"! The closing ceremonies seemed like a Hollywood production to me — the national officers were like beauty pageant winners, and were even more impressive on stage! The lighting and presentations were like nothing I'd ever seen at a dental meeting! My ABWA chapter, the Soaring Eagles, had our moment in the sun also, with our chapter winning a coveted Star award, and our entire southern California contingent dancing on stage in purple suits to promote the following year's meeting in Anaheim.

While serving as program chair in my local chapter, it was my goal to find speakers who would enrich our group through education. I believe that often what we avoid doing is what prevents us from achieving our personal goals. Many women, including me, dislike public speaking; but to be successful in our careers, developing good communication skills is vital. I scheduled a public speaking coach to visit our chapter, and brought in experts in marketing, personal safety and fitness. Education often provides the stepping stone that gets us past our personal obstacles and with supportive business women colleagues to encourage us, there is no better place than ABWA to improve and practice new skills.

ABWA has taught me many important business skills, such as how to network better. I came to understand the strength that many women have, and take advantage of to build their businesses by developing relationships. I learned other subtleties of networking, such as asking for favors (and donations) from business people I deal with and helping them feel good about it. I reached out more in the business community, within the chamber of commerce and elsewhere, such as in non-profit groups. I have tried to emulate the best qualities of the many amazing women I have encountered. I learned that ABWA members are mentors and don't hesitate to enthusiastically give and receive positive feedback. I learned to recognize different leadership and communication styles and the advantages of each. We don't compete with each other; in fact, we enhance the unique skills each of us has through positive support for each other. Our diverse occupations and backgrounds are always interesting and provide great opportunities for growth that isn't always available within our own professions.

A few years ago, after 20 years in practice and an increasingly filling schedule, I found myself evaluating my life and realizing that the hectic pace of combining work and family had squeezed out time for many of my personal interests. I would not describe it as career burnout, but something closer to a mid-life crisis. With four sons to raise and educate and a new house under construction, I didn't see retirement on the near horizon. I wanted a sabbatical! I value free time, and I felt that I just didn't have enough of it. I wanted "me" time.

I started planning for my break about six months in advance, mentoring a new woman dentist whom we had known for a few years. She agreed to work part time to cover my patients and some of my days in the office. I wanted to be off work for six months, and scheduled March through September for my planned time frame. My staff was very supportive, but I was undecided whether to officially notify my patients. For six months, most would not realize my absence. After telling one patient of my plan, I did not receive a positive response, so I concluded that explaining my intentions to my patients was not a good idea!

Many people advised me to write out a schedule of my plans: I felt the opposite. I was tired of being constantly scheduled and wanted the freedom to choose how to spend my time. I didn't set big goals for myself, because I wanted to see how being spontaneous felt! With my children in school the first three months, I spent time organizing my personal space, sleeping in, reading and actually relaxing. I didn't account for or schedule much of my time, but I did spend a week as a summer Cub Scout Day Camp leader. With several other part-time parent volunteers to assist me, it went well until my co-leader developed pregnancy complications and was absent for the major part of the week. I now had twice as many young Scouts to manage, and the challenge became exhausting. By the time I finished the week, I not only wanted a vacation, I was "over" my sense of obligation to serve as a leader.

I scheduled a 10 day trip alone back to my home town. During this escape, I planned a get-together with high school friends who I rarely had time to see. I explored all over town, and spent most days with a close friend who was a teacher and had summers off. At last I felt I was finding myself again! During that summer, I wanted to experience some activities I had never tried. Some of my experiences included volunteering with a Billy Graham Crusade in San Diego and serving on jury duty for the first time. While both were unique opportunities for me, I decided that I'd prefer to delay the jury duty again until I really retire!

For the first time in many years, I had regained the freedom to plan my time any way I wanted, and by September, I was ready to return to work, with some new ideas and plans for how I wanted to spend the rest of my life. I learned how to focus my time better, and to build in time to do things that mattered to me. I realized that the one who suffered the most from over scheduling was me, and that I was responsible for my own physical and mental well-being. I have seen too many women allow themselves to be so buried in responsibility for others that they don't take enough time for themselves. A break from work, when planned in advance, can be a great opportunity to re-charge! I am so grateful that I did not have to experience a medical or family crisis for this to happen.

My career as a healthcare professional and business owner has provided great variety and challenge for me. I have been able to satisfy my artistic, creative side and my analytical traits as well. I have enjoyed being able to meet the needs of the patients I care for, and in many cases, help to improve their self image and quality of life. I have also found fulfillment in life through education, involvement in community organizations and developing new friendships. I know that the relationships that intertwine my work with my personal life are among the ones that enrich my life the most deeply. My friendships with my ABWA sisters will impact me for the rest of my life!

Epilogue

I have found my year as the 2008 American Business Woman of ABWA to be like nothing I have ever experienced. The good will and enthusiastic support I have received within ABWA and in my own community have far surpassed my expectations. I have come to understand that this honorary position is primarily the role of an ambassador. Wherever I have gone with ABWA, from district and national conferences to regional council programs, my experiences have always been unique and energizing. As I have met many ABWA members from across the country since Greensborough, I have concluded that it's important to strengthen our bonds with other businesswomen. We don't always know how the connections we make will impact us in our lives, but I know that my ABWA friendships have enriched my life immensely.

In ABWA and in our personal lives, we all have opportunities to act as mentors and coaches to others. It has been my goal this year to encourage women to keep learning and growing, and connecting through ABWA. As we connect with other women, I believe we can offer them many unique growth opportunities through involvement in ABWA. Through this year, my travels and experiences have enabled me to connect with members and non-members, to network, encourage and to celebrate our diversity as unique and talented businesswomen.

The 2008 Top Tens are a diverse group who share many common bonds. We are all accomplished in our careers, and are proud of our ABWA membership and our fellow members' achievements. I am amazed and humbled to read the stories of the women who joined me as Top Tens this year. Many of their life challenges and detours have been beyond my comprehension, but through their own personal strength and support systems, they overcame them! In creating their own personal "success stories" each of these women has become adept at doing what needs to be done. They have developed outstanding careers while providing financial support to their families and service to their communities. I hope that these women's stories will be as inspiring to others as they have been to me.

Richie B. Morris

Living Our Dreams

As a Top Ten Business Woman of the American Business Women's Association, I am living my dream — a dream filled with joy, love and gratitude. How joyous it is to gain national recognition for serving from the heart — and the honor is that much sweeter because I have not served to be honored, I have been honored to serve.

However, I must admit that I have dreamed of becoming a Top Ten since attending my first Top Ten luncheon. Members of my Hidden Hills chapter and I discussed becoming a Top Ten at our table as we listened to the fascinating stories shared by ten incredible women seven years ago. Each year I look forward to hearing the Top Ten speeches at our national conference, so when my ABWA mentor, Gwendolyn West, encouraged me to become a candidate, I complied. She was convinced that my credentials qualified as Top Ten.

Words can not adequately describe my elation when the national president notified me of this prestigious honor. It was a moment which I shall never forget, a moment that I recall frequently. It included the huge scream that my sister bellowed when I shared my wonderful news. I was sitting in my cube at Delta Airlines and I couldn't make the scream for myself at the time. I kept my composure and continued a lovely conversation with Robin. My life has not been the same and my heart is filled with gratitude for Gwendolyn West and for all of the servant leaders who have blazed the trails before me.

I have an attitude of gratitude for the shoulders of so many true servant leaders upon which I stand — true servant leaders who exude true leadership and exemplify true success. For example, Gwendolyn is a past Atlanta area council chair and is employed full time. She became the first African American female bailiff in Dekalb County Georgia. She is a wife, mother, grandmother, big sister, caregiver to both mother and father, actively works in the church and the community, and always providing excellent and fun presentations at ABWA events. Somehow she manages time to mentor.

Gwendolyn firmly believes that "to whom much is given, much is expected." She does not just "talk the talk," she "walks the walk" and actually walks the talk.

When I connected with ABWA I was most fortunate to reconnect with her. We became close friends while attending Spelman College in Atlanta, Georgia. Gwendolyn worked in the registrar's office and served as a young role model to all of her sisters. She was then and remains today a professional business woman.

During the late '60s and early '70s, Gwendolyn donned her white crisp shirts, stockings, blazers, and skirts and carried a stenographer's pad while most of us looked like hippies. She could easily rest on her well deserved laurels; however, this truly successful leader works very hard to groom successors and celebrates with us when we exceed.

The Atlanta Area Council thrives because of true servant leaders like Gwendolyn West, leaders who equip members with the necessary tools to engage, experience and excel. Each year the mantle of success is passed to those who continue to raise the bar, true to our ABWA mission. I am eternally grateful to them and to my loving and closely knit family for impacting my success.

Moreover, I thank my husband, Henry Morris, for his consistent and generous support as he has eagerly assisted me with projects for the past 33 years. Furthermore, he is a great hairstylist and image consultant, ensuring that my image is always professional. His confidence in me is enormous, and Henry knows the importance of image and that impressions are lasting.

My brilliant and loving father, Russell Brown, deserves acknowledging, along with his awesome mother, Mama Maude. My father became a young single parent of three small children after our mother died when I was only two years old. My 32 year old father vowed to keep his young children together although he could have given us to loving family members. My father and his mother sacrificed tremendously to make sure that our home was filled with love and learning and our bond has never been broken. My sister, Maude, has been the perfect friend, role model, Big Spelman Sister, and ABWA Sister. My brother Edd, continues to be a major source of motivation. Passions for learning, loving and laughing were instilled in me at an early age and those passions make ABWA a perfect venue for my skills and personality.

When I accepted the invitation to attend the Hidden Hills Chapter meeting from my neighbor, Pauline Dailey, I had no prior knowledge of this great association and I did not know any of the members. However, I joined the same evening and I have not missed a meeting in nearly eight years. My loyal service has been greatly rewarded as I have supported the goals of individual members and the mission of ABWA. I was honored as the Atlanta Area Council 2007 Woman of the Year. I have served as president of the Hidden Hills Chapter and as Woman of the Year.

I am a Charter Member of the Atlanta Downtown Express Network (ADEN) and reigned as the 2006 ADEN Woman of the Year. I am honored to serve as ADEN'S President Elect and look forward to leading this premiere network. I have missed only one ADEN meeting in five years due to a schedule conflict caused by a training class that my employer asked me to attend.

As president of the Hidden Hills Chapter, we earned the Star Award and celebrated an unprecedented year which included a National Newsletter Award and recognition from national for a successful joint gala. I am a member of the Inner Circle with 19 sponsored members. After my first year I have attended each National Conference with full registration and at least one Spring Conference.

The education and the skills that I have honed in ABWA make me a valuable asset in every area of my life. I am a charter member of the Stone Mountain Chapter of the National Association of Spelman Alumni and enjoy the title of being their "largest fund raiser."

Applying what I have learned in ABWA, I offer great suggestions for my fellow Spelman Sisters as we grow our chapter. I also achieve success as the Vice President of Education for Delta Airlines Premiere Toastmasters by applying what I have learned in ABWA and find the missions are similar. Having achieved lifetime membership with Weight Watchers, I find similarities there as well and have been invited to join their staff. My growth in ABWA also helps me serve in the women's ministry at Messiah's House Assembly of God in Stone Mountain, Georgia where I teach Sunday School and narrate holiday programs and special events.

When the Hidden Hills Chapter celebrated its tenth anniversary I invited Congresswoman Cynthia McKinney to be one of our special guests. She was so impressed with ABWA that she joined, sponsored many new members, and requested that we help organize a volunteer appreciation event. Her staff was so pleased that they offered me a position and I was promoted from staff assistant to constituent representative within a year. As a constituent representative I organized six town hall meetings assisting seniors with Medicare prescription drug plans, international business leader meetings, assisted constituents with Social Security benefits, food stamps, child support, immigrations and civic association receptions. I am a consultant with Tarrah Cosmetics, an aloe based company for skincare, healthcare, and wellness and frequently use these products to pamper senior citizens.

My education includes a Bachelor of Arts degree from Spelman College, a Master's degree in Special Education from Atlanta University (Clark Atlanta University) and a Cosmetology License. I have taught public school in Duval County Florida and Clayton County Georgia. My career with Delta Airlines spans 27years with numerous contract assignments since retirement.

Many years at Delta were spent in basic reservations sales and customer service. I became a facilitator, training new hires, attorneys, general directors, executives and recurrent Delta employees. I received many compliments from customers and fellow employees. I joined the Delta Pioneers and I enjoy numerous speaker programs on the Delta Campus sponsored by various employee networks. In my virtual ABWA handbook my picture is after the mission because I have taken full advantage of the networking and educational benefits which have groomed me for true success and have inspired me to give back and to give forward.

During my Top Ten interview I was asked what is it that I am most proud of and I immediately spoke from my heart. My response was the sincere support and joy that fellow members display for my success. I strongly recommend reading Rick Warren's *Purpose Driven Life* with a partner and discussing the questions in each chapter. Answer the questions with someone that you trust and who wants you to fulfill your destiny. My ABWA sponsor, Pauline ,did this with me and our lives have become much richer for this experience.

If you have not read the writings of Florence Scovil Schinn, please do. Her book, *The Game of Life and How to Play It,* may change your life as well. Schinn uses the term "metaphysics" which are really "old school" teachings such as "do unto others as you would have them do unto you", and follow the "golden rule," or biblical teachings such as "you reap what you sow." The book teaches that everything we do comes back to us, and when it returns it comes back multiplied, good or bad. Not only does this apply to our deeds, but also our words. We will have what we say

— our words are not void. Our words are our wands. When we change our words, we change our world. When we change our thinking, we change our lives.

ABWA love and fellowship motivate me to help members achieve true success by fulfilling their purpose driven lives — to encourage positive self-images, and positive as well as grateful attitudes. I know that as long as one has a poor self-image it doesn't matter how much one achieves. That person will never feel successful and will chase titles and wealth without ever realizing a sense of accomplishment. Truly successful ABWA Members feel successful. It is our "attitude and not our aptitude that determines our altitude" (author unknown). I know the importance of attitude in life and how it affects success. True success can be guaranteed by maintaining a positive attitude toward every ABWA member and every situation.

Too many people are resenters, resisters or regreters, resisting everything. They are energy drainers. We must roll with those who celebrate us as we do in ABWA — not merely tolerate us. Resenters, resisters and regreters are not living in the now. We must live unafraid in the now.

I know the importance of a "can do attitude." "If you think you can or if you think you can't, you are right." (author unknown).

I am reminded of my favorite quote regarding attitude and I feel that it is worth sharing.

Attitude

"The longer I live, the more I realize the impact of attitude on life. Attitude to me is more important than the facts. It is more important than the past, than education, money, than circumstances, than failures, than successes, than what other people think or say or do. It is more important than appearance, giftedness or skill. It will make or break a relationship, a business, or a home. The remarkable thing is that we have a choice every day regarding the attitude we will embrace for that day. We cannot change our past. We cannot change the inevitable. The only thing we can do is play on the one thing we can change for the better...our attitude. I am convinced that life is 10 percent what happens to us and 90 percent how we react to it. We are each in charge of our own attitudes and how we deal with our customers, our peers, our families and our friends each day."(Dr. Charles Swindoll, President, Dallas Theological Seminary)

As truly successful ABWA members, we have mastered the art of balancing time: the past, the present and the future. Truly successful ABWA members know when to honor the past, forge the future, and enjoy the gift of the present. As truly successful members of ABWA we know how to learn from the past so we do not repeat mistakes which become larger when they are not learned. We know how to build upon the past and we know when to let go of it. We know how to move forward. We know how to plan for the future with written goals, action plans and time lines. We know that when we fail to plan, we plan to fail.

However, truly successful ABWA members know that we cannot spend so much time planning the future that we do not live each day to the fullest. We know that what we do today determines our future. We need to live the Serenity Prayer knowing that we can not change the past. Truly successful members do not allow fear to keep us in the past, whether it is fear of failure or even worse, fear of success.

We cannot become too content in our comfort zones. Sometimes we must fight through the fear and do what we have to do even if we are afraid when we are doing it.

Often fear (F-E-A-R) is false evidence appearing real, according to minister Joyce Meyers. Too often it is finding excuses and reasons (Bessie Poole). Procrastination is another word for fear. Fear of failure and humiliation are understandable and when we know that we are doing the right things for the right reasons in the right seasons, we must stay determined. Even when we lose we don't really lose if we don't lose the lesson.

When we lose we know more ways of how to not do something. Thomas Edison had faith in the laws of electricity. He knew what could be done with it if it were harnessed and directed. After years of patient, loving absorption in his work despite being discouraged by everyone, including his own father, electric lights illuminate the world.

We can harness and direct our thoughts. There are many inventers and many success stories of how long and how hard they worked before their goals and dreams were realized.

"That which does not destroy us makes us stronger." I have become so secure in ABWA that I have learned how to laugh at myself rather than becoming humiliated. Laughter is literally a great medicine. Now when I make a mistake I can laugh with those who really are laughing at me. People say they are laughing with us — not at us. Don't believe it. The reason something seems so funny is because it is happening to you and not to them.

In addition, another roadblock to moving forward is not being able to forgive. Truly successful ABWA members forgive. We forgive those who have hurt us and we forgive ourselves. We let go of the past and we give ourselves the gift of forgiveness (Rev. Charles Stanley).

We become better and not bitter. We do not relinquish our power to others. By forgiving we do not allow others to live rent free in our minds. Studies have found that not forgiving causes disease in our bodies. Joyce Meyers believes that "unforgiveness is like killing someone with poison but we drink the poison."

As truly successful ABWA members we make wise choices. We choose to operate our lives like well-driven automobiles — moving forward whenever possible, but using the rear view mirror when we need to back up as we sometimes do in life to move in the right direction.

A passage in ***Chicken Soup For the Soul*** by Jack Canfield reads, "The past is gone but now is forever. The future lies in the hands of the present." (Chicken Soup for the Soul Publishing, LLC)

Our destination is a life-long journey towards true success. I strongly encourage each of us to honor the past, forge the future, accept, unwrap and enjoy the gift of the present by living each day to the fullest. Dream as Mr. Hilary Bufton, Jr. dreamed of better working conditions for women when the term business woman was an oddity and an association for business women was unheard of.

Act upon your dream and live your dream. My father dreamed of keeping his three small children together and acted upon his dream. Dr. Martin Luther King, Jr. dreamed. He organized and acted upon his dream which continues to change the world for the better, 40 years after his murder. We know that dreams without goals are merely wishes.

In addition to making New Year resolutions, let's make New Year realizations. Paul Meyer states that "identity is the strongest force in the human psyche." We must be authentic and true to self. By taking advantage of the great education, networking and fellowship opportunities in ABWA, my life has changed drastically for the better.

I am no longer a "people pleaser" and I have learned

how to say no. I am no longer easily manipulated. I no longer have to be the all and do all. I no longer have to attend every event. I can now ask myself what is the main event and choose. Too many of us are over scheduled. Truly successful members of ABWA have learned how to leave time for rest and how to stay healthy.

Having said that, I will add that I was the baby all of my life and that I was only two when my mother died. My family unknowingly contributed to me becoming easily manipulated, my inability to say no, and my desire to please. They overcompensated for my mother's death when I was so young by constantly labeling me the baby and by treating me like a baby. On the positive side, this has also made me a loving nurturer, always willing to share and to help.

Although I would deny being a baby, I must have subconsciously believed I was. All of us are who we believe what was said about us when we were very young and what we internalized. This is why it is imperative to guard what we say to small children.

I strongly encourage each of you to think back to your earliest memories of what was said about you. If those titles were negative, you owe it to yourself to work on those thoughts if you have not overcome the labels of the past.

In conclusion, it is my desire for each of us to realize our destiny and purpose, to live our dreams. However, we must deal with our "stuff" — our unresolved issues, our behavioral patterns, gifts, talents, values, visions, dreams and love. Constance Arnold says "when we don't deal with our stuff, our stuff deals with us."

Not only do I now know who I am now but I embrace my uniqueness; I love myself and I celebrate my success. As a truly successful member of ABWA, I celebrate with those who are dear to me and I honor those who have helped me become successful. I know that today is the first day of the rest of my life and I am determined to make the rest of my life the best of my life.

In addition to living each day to the fullest, we must remember that every deed is a seed. Whatever we do comes back to us, and when it comes back it is multiplied.

Finally, I will continue to help members discover their inner Ten in them, or whatever it is they dream of becoming and to heed the words of Paul Meyer. "Whatever you vividly imagine, ardently desire, sincerely believe and enthusiastically act upon, must inevitably come to pass."

Sweet dreams!

Epilogue

The 2009 Top Tens have been selected and the end of our current reign is fast approaching. Basking in the adulation of Top Ten has been phenomenal. Being proudly recognized at every ABWA event, apprised of ABWA news before it is released to the general public, invited to speak at meetings, asked to install executive boards, and sharing our stories and receiving the royal treatment at conferences have contributed to this year of "DREAMS FULFILLED" — my dreams and those of my father, Mr. Russell Brown, ABWA Founder, Mr. Hilary Bufton, Jr. and the Reverend Dr. Martin Luther King, Jr.

When I share my Top Ten Story I pay homage to ABWA founder, Mr. Hilary Bufton, Jr. who dreamed of better working conditions for women before women became a viable part of the American workforce. I honor my father, Mr. Russell Brown who dreamed of keeping his three small children together when our mother died. Only 32 years old, he acted upon his dream and our bonds have not been broken. My brother, Edd, my sister, Maude, and I credit my father with much of our success because he never let a day go by without showing us how much he loved us and how proud he was of us. He provided for us and inspired us to pursue our dreams. Finally, I remember the Reverend Dr. Martin Luther King, Jr. who dreamed of civil rights for everyone. These great humanitarians acted upon their dreams decades ago and as a result the world continues to become better.

I have spent this year encouraging others to live their dreams, to act upon their dreams and to remember that dreams without goals are merely wishes. Because I acted upon my dream of becoming a Top Ten, I am an ABWA Ambassador, a "Forever Ten," giving back and paying forward, sowing and reaping the benefits of ABWA Servant Leadership.

I encourage people to choose to be better instead of bitter when faced with negativity. For those who have made the mistake of adhering to the adage of "don't get mad, get even" — please stop! Do not continue to be your own worst enemy. Feel free to get mad as there are advantages to getting mad. But for your sake, do not get even. Get better. One little letter can make the giant difference between bitter and better. Because I chose better instead of bitter, I am truly enjoying the "time of my life": older, wiser and better.

I am young enough to still enjoy true success and energetic enough to influence the success of others. I am old enough to know that women in the United States of America have come a very long way in not very many years. I am old enough to know that we have come a long way but young enough to know that we still have a very long way to go. I am old enough to have attended segregated schools in Jacksonville, Florida and young enough to remember the "whites only" signs.

I was the guest speaker at an ABWA Meeting on the anniversary of the "Women's Right to Vote." As I helped celebrate the progress of women, I also thought of how I could not have been served in that restaurant not so long ago simply because of my skin color. In addition, I thought to myself how awesome it is that I joined ABWA only eight years ago and now I am accepting speaking requests. My virtual ABWA dictionary contains a picture of me next to our ABWA Mission Statement ("...to bring together businesswomen of diverse occupations and to provide opportunities for them to help themselves and others grow personally and professionally through leadership, education, networking support and national recognition…").

Fortunately, I chose to accept my ABWA sponsor Pauline Dailey's invitation to attend the Hidden Hills Chapter of ABWA and past National Secretary Treasurer Teresa Williams' request to become a Charter Member of the Atlanta Downtown Express Network (ADEN) of ABWA. I am honored to serve as the current President of ADEN. My visions and my dreams for ADEN members are enormous. I confidently "Promise to Deliver (this year's national theme)" because ABWA delivers when we focus on our mission and our members. In addition to serving ADEN, I am the Co-Chair of Education for the Atlanta Area Council of ABWA, Education Vice President of Delta (Airlines) Premier Toastmasters, Parliamentarian of the Stone Mountain, Georgia Chapter of the National Alumni Association for Spelman College, an active member in the Women's Ministry of Messiah's House Church in Stone Mountain, Georgia, and I have recently been employed by Weight Watchers. I have been blessed with unlimited opportunities for assisting others with living their dreams.

The number eight signifies "new beginning" and 2008 has truly been a wonderful new beginning for my life. Consider the following great eights I have experienced: I am a 2008 Top Ten. I was selected during my 8th year of membership in ABWA. On the 88th Anniversary of Women's

Rights, I celebrated the progress of women and equal rights for all. And, in the 8th month, on the 28th day, in the year of 2008 (08-28-08), it was my husband Henry's birthday.

In 2008, the dreams of my father, Mr. Bufton, and Dr. King were realized in America.

Together our family watched the acceptance speech of an African American as a presidential nominee. A female received more than 18 million votes for president.

A female was selected as the running mate for vice president. Age, gender, race and religion are no longer barriers for presidential candidates.

As an older African American female, I witnessed dreams fulfilled, which I did not expect to see during my lifetime. In Dr. King's "I Have a Dream" speech, delivered at the March on Washington 45 years earlier to the day that an African American candidate delivered his acceptance speech as the presidential nominee of his party, Dr. King spoke of letting freedom ring from the Rockies of Colorado to the Stone Mountain of Georgia. My sister, Maude and her husband, Kevin, reside in Colorado. They participated in the recent historic events there and arrived at our home in Stone Mountain, Georgia minutes before the presidential candidate made his acceptance speech.

Though racism and discrimination exist today, our hope has been renewed and we celebrate our progress. Together we all dream bigger dreams. We all act upon our dreams and we all fulfill our purpose driven lives by divine design.

Marcita Scharnhorst

Eleanor Roosevelt said, "You must do the things you think you cannot do."

She was an inspiration for women and way ahead of her time. Eleanor Roosevelt helped pave the way for women to be respected and admired as professionals in business, and not just in the traditional housewife role that was expected of women of that era.

Life is a journey that begins with birth. The challenges and obstacles that we encounter along that journey help to develop our characters and form the individuals that we become.

My life began when I was born as the fourth child to German parents in Kansas. My youth was typical of most families in that area participating in school activities, 4-H, pep club, FHA, square dancing, etc. Growing up in a large family, we were all expected to do our share of the chores and work together. I learned early how to work and how important family and friends were in our lives. After graduation from high school, I moved several hundred miles away to attend business college. Being away from home, I realized how much I missed those close family ties and quickly I moved from being a teenager to an adult on this early part of my journey. My first job after graduation from business school was to work on a military base for a missile contractor in human resources. This is where I met my husband and when he finished his tour in the military, we moved to Georgia, his home. This move took me even further away from family and friends.

With my early close family ties and personality of a person who must be involved and busy, living in Georgia away from family during the long winter months offered a new challenge in life. It was during this time that I needed to do something to occupy my time and went to work in Atlanta for a temporary agency. Working part-time allowed me more work flexibility to arrange my schedule around family needs. It was quite a challenge to learn to maneuver my way around the city since I came from a small town out west. One of my jobs with the temporary agency led me to a position at the Presbyterian Center. This eventually led to full time employment that lasted nearly five years. Eventually I grew to dislike the twenty-five mile one-way commute and started looking for a job closer to home.

A neighbor told me about a job at GreyStone – an electric membership corporation, or EMC — that was one mile from my home, and is still my current employer. My first job was working in the Information Systems Department. I really grew up with this organization and have remained here for 35 years. When I started, we only had about 75 employees and 40,000 consumers.

GreyStone Power Corporation is a non-profit electric utility located in Douglasville, Georgia. The Board of Directors is the governing body of the organization. The President/CEO answers to the Board and the Board answers to the members it serves. There are approximately 1,000 EMCs around the country that primarily serve rural areas. Today, we are the 19th largest EMC in the country with nearly 100,000 consumers and 300 employees. GreyStone continues to experience seven percent growth annually as one of the fastest growing EMCs in the U.S., with annual revenues reaching $200 million.

The next ten years I spent raising my three sons and doing all the things parents do participating in kids' activities: baseball, football, basketball, chorus and scouts (I was a den mother). Slowly my journey began to change course as I was beginning to face marital problems.

A few years later I found myself going through a difficult divorce. Divorce was not something that happened in my family and was quite difficult for my father to accept, especially since he lived 1,500 miles away. Being the major supporter of my family, I began to realize that I needed more education to move ahead in my career. I studied and planned to take the college entrance exam in the fall of the late 1970s. I passed the exam and began taking classes but the nearest college that offered night classes was more than 30 miles away. Twice a week after working an eight hour day, I headed to class. With no family close by, I had to depend on friends to help with the children. Sometimes when I came home late from class at night my youngest son, who was still in high school, would still be waiting up for me. Friends became my support system.

After attending class for five years, I finally had earned enough credits to have completed one year of college. By this time all my three sons were in college around different parts of the country. I learned to handle almost any crisis myself, from doing yard maintenance, home repairs and even some car repairs. These life experiences strengthened my character and increased my desire to reach higher up the ladder to become more self-sufficient.

In the fall of 1983 my life completely changed its course when a dear friend encouraged me to take up square dancing for entertainment. This is where I met this great guy who is my wonderful husband still today. We were about the same age, loved square dancing and actually grew up fairly close to each other out west. The relationship was destined to be from the beginning. We both came from old German families and had a great deal in common. We married within a year and combined our families with now five children all in college.

My career with GreyStone Power just kept humming along. In 1984, I applied for a position in the human resources department managing payroll and benefits. This change was the best career move that I ever made and set the path of my journey in my career to where I am today. My husband was the one who encouraged me to apply for the job and make the change. I always thought that I would work in the human resources job for a few years, and when a position opened up for an accounting manager I would apply and go back to accounting which is where I had worked for ten years. When the position did open up a few years later, I discussed applying for the position with the CEO of GreyStone Power but he told me that I wasn't qualified because I did not have a degree. I told him that I was going to school and would graduate in a couple of years. He told me that I would never make it.

I had dropped out of school temporarily when I married to begin my life with my new family. However, I still had this nagging dream to one day complete my education. After a couple of years, my husband encouraged me to get back in school because he knew how important it was for me to accomplish my dream. This time with his support, I transferred to another college closer to home that offered more night classes. I really just intended to get my associate degree but when the time came, I just kept going. The struggle to attend classes at night, work an eight hour day, and find family time was difficult. My oldest son, who was attending college close by and had continued to live at home, became my tutor through algebra classes. During my last two years of college I was on the dean's or president's list almost every quarter.

Five years after going back to school for the second time, I finally graduated from Kennesaw College in Marietta, Georgia in 1992. No words can describe how it felt to walk across that stage and to finally realize my dream to be a college graduate. There had been many obstacles to overcome and sometimes I wasn't sure if I would make it or not, but each time I reached a milestone that brought me closer to my dream, I got charged to work harder. I was a much stronger person when I accepted my diploma and nothing could take away the sense of achievement and pride that I felt when I walked across the stage. My husband and three sons were especially proud of me and were all there for the great celebration.

My husband was a real trooper during my years of attending classes and kept the house running which allowed me the time to focus on homework and class assignments. However, in 1989 a series of circumstances almost destroyed our dreams. Within a three month period of time, I had major surgery, my oldest son married, our home burned, and my youngest son married. His wedding was scheduled for a date three weeks after the house burned and all of our clothing was destroyed. The week before the wedding, my husband told me to go shopping and not to come home until I had a dress. The first dress that I had purchased for the wedding had been destroyed in the fire.

Can you imagine what it's like to wake up one day and have no clothes to wear, no toothbrush and no place to live? I gained a new appreciation for the wonderful life that God had given me. I had so much to be thankful for that no one was injured and we survived the fire because the firemen told us we were lucky the fire was during the day. We would never have survived the fire if it had broken out during the night because it started in our bedroom and spread very quickly throughout the house. During this time I stayed in school, we moved to an apartment for three months. I continued to work full time and we survived and became even stronger human beings.

I don't remember too much about the last wedding after the fire but I was there dressed as the mother of the groom — somehow.

While struggling to attend classes and pay for my education, I didn't know about ABWA and the scholarships that it makes available to women. As ABWA leaders, we must do a better job to educate our members and individuals in our communities about the educational opportunities that

ABWA offers its members. Offering scholarships to women offers a great opportunity to help them finance their education. Sometimes this is the only funding that they have to complete their education.

Graduating from college was just the beginning of a new career and life was wonderful. I was on a roll and wanted to continue to learn more. I took classes through our local technical school to enhance my computer skills. I wanted to know more about the legal requirements of administering payroll, human resources and benefits. I learned about the American Payroll Association in Atlanta and joined that organization. Through APA I began to prepare for the National Certified Payroll Professional exam to become a Certified Payroll Professional (CPP). I passed the test on the first attempt. The National average for participants to pass this exam on the first attempt was about 64 percent. I later went on to teach classes with APA on benefits and payroll processing to members preparing for the exam. I also joined the Society of Human Resource Management (SHRM) and a few years later begin the process to sit for the national exam to earn certification as a Professional in Human Resources (PHR). This required taking a series of classes to prepare for the exam. I also passed it at the first attempt.

In the early 1990s the economy was bad and electric utilities were facing possible deregulation. GreyStone Power had implemented a hiring freeze that had been in place for two years. Managers made the decision to bring in a consultant to reorganize the company in preparation for deregulation. The entire process was poorly handled which resulted in ten employees scheduled to be terminated. Layoffs had never occurred before in the 65-year history of the organization. Our board of directors changed the directive and ordered the employees to be transferred to other jobs within the organization. The HR department had to prepare severance packages in case some of those employees refused the transfer and chose to accept the severance packages offered to them. Six of the employees left the organization. Terminating these employees was a difficult assignment for me and I cried during the process. My manager told me I needed to get used to it if I ever planned to manage the Human Resource Department. The whole process destroyed the morale of the entire organization that took years to repair the damage caused by the study.

As a payroll manager my career with GreyStone was also in jeopardy. I wasn't sure what my job would be when the dust settled. While on a family vacation my manager contacted me and strongly suggested that I needed to return to Georgia early for a Monday morning meetings. Payroll was moved to accounting along with the payroll clerk. I had a job but not as a manager. This arrangement lasted for a couple of years and when the employee later resigned, payroll was returned to human resources.

In 1994, a friend invited me to attend an ABWA meeting with her. I quickly became hooked on this organization and wished many times that I had known about ABWA years before. I was amazed at all the wonderful women I met through the organization and continued to be immensely impressed by how involved and dedicated ABWA members are. The first year after joining ABWA, I was asked to serve on the board and continue that practice today. I sort of fell into leadership roles and realized one day how much this organization built my self confidence and self esteem. It was natural that new leadership skills came with the program. Each year new opportunities arose and doors opened that I never dreamed possible.

The 42 electric membership corporations in the state of Georgia have an organization of human resources and administrative executive personnel around the state. This organization sponsors two conferences each year, and for many years I attended these meetings. Being involved with this organization gave me the opportunity to network and become acquainted with other human resources managers. In recent years, these professionals have provided a huge support group to me when I took over the human resources department at GreyStonc Power. Later I served in leadership roles of this organization and still reside on that board today.

Another resource that EMCs have access to is the National Rural Electric Cooperative (NRECA) that is based in Arlington, VA. This organization provides training, benefits and many other services and resources to EMCs in the United States. I started attending National Benefit and Human Resource Conferences early in my career with GreyStone Power. It was through this organization and the contacts that I established that I was asked to serve on a national insurance task force to review benefits and to determine what changes should occur with benefits that NRECA provided to EMCs around the United States. This committee resulted in many changes in benefits for EMCs. The task force recommendations resulted in changes that moved benefits for EMCs from the traditional indemnity plan to managed care organizations within the medical insurance industry.

Joining ABWA opened doors and charted the journey that I am on today. While serving in leadership roles and as president of ABWA, my leadership abilities were being recognized by community leaders. This recognition led to appointments to the CORE Board, Atlanta Regional Workforce Board, Cultural Art Center Board and the Chamber of Commerce Accreditation Committee. This relationship with the CAC led to the partnership with ABWA to co-sponsor an annual event called the "Mad Hatters Tea Party" which gives us great exposure in the community and has brought new members to our chapter.

In 1999 the Manger of Human Resources at GreyStone Power retired. At the same time the President/CEO of the organization announced his plans to retire within six months. EMCs are an industry that tends to have few female executives in their organizations. I knew there was a male in our organization who would be jockeying for the HR manager's position when she retired. I was thrilled to be appointed as the acting manager of the human resource department during the interim until the new CEO was announced. I wasn't too sure that I would get the position that I had worked and prepared for over so many years. However, after serving for six months in this position, I was awarded the manager's position. With all good things come difficulty and the road was not smooth in the transition. Several employees in the department quit. One of my ABWA friends came to my rescue and worked for me for about six months until I could get employees hired and trained. The positive side is that I could build my own team of employees in the human resources department. All of the employees that were hired during this time still work with me today.

During this same time, my personal life suffered a huge blow. The worst nightmare of any parent's life happened to our family. It was the kind of thing that happens to other people, not nice families like ours. My two year old granddaughter was kidnapped by her father. Law enforcement didn't consider it kidnapping because our daughter wasn't yet divorced from the baby's father. They considered it a domestic dispute. We immediately moved our daughter and her other two children into our home.

Amber alerts were not being used then. They would have been a godsend during this time to help us recover our granddaughter. I really believe that if amber alerts were being used in 1999, she would have been found much sooner. Law enforcement officials warned us it might take years to find the baby. We would not accept that news. We were determined not to give up looking for our granddaughter. Our family, along with law enforcement agencies in the area, searched for her for nearly five months. We personally tracked every lead ourselves and contacted the baby's father's family members, who refused to cooperate. We contacted every credit agency that we knew he was connected with. It was through these efforts that our granddaughter was finally located in Washington. Ford Motor Credit notified the local police department that his vehicle was picked up in a suburb of Seattle.

My ABWA friends formed a huge support team to assist our family. When things get tough, we appreciate the real meaning of friendships and I was reminded of how important family and friends are to our wellbeing and existence in life. We never know what struggles life will throw our way but the hard times that we endure shapes the individuals that we become in life, stronger and more compassionate human beings.

I had been the Department Manager of Human Resources for about a year when my boss came to me in late 2000 and said there was something that he needed me to take care of. Of course I offered my support to help with his problem, as always. It was then that he told me he was going to make me a Vice President, but it had to be kept a secret until he was ready to make the announcement. This promotion made me the first female to ever serve on the Executive Team in the history of GreyStone Power Corporation. I had cracked the glass ceiling. My journey just turned a sharp curve and would offer many new challenges for me to conquer.

Some of my responsibilities at GreyStone Power include the promotion of wellness programs. In 2004, we received one of four wellness awards that were given to companies throughout metro Atlanta that "support a healthy workforce." GreyStone Power received first place in the Promina Corporate Challenge for our wellness program among companies with 100 to 200 employees. 600 companies participated in this event. This past year we promoted a Weight Watchers' program for employees and our retirees. We had consultants with Weight Watchers come to our organization to run the classes. During the 24-week program, we had about 65 employees participate. The group lost over 1,400 pounds. Weight Watchers corporate were so impressed with the success of our program that we were featured in their corporate newsletter.

I directed our organization through the first ever employee survey conducted by an outside consultant. Managers at GreyStone had conducted their own survey about 15 years before, but never communicated the results to employees because they didn't like the comments and the results of the survey. The goal of this survey was to determine how our employees felt about the organization. We asked questions about their likes and dislikes and about the management team. We communicated the results to employees, good and bad. It was from this survey that I was instructed to lead another organizational study. This was a dangerous move because of the disastrous study done 10 years before. It had to be handled in a professional manner. We brought in four consultants who were associated with our industry from various parts of the country to handle the study. They conducted interviews with managers and key employees. The last step was to bring all managers and employees together to communicate the results. There were no secrets. Everything was open and communicated. Few changes were made as a direct result of the study, but it was determined that several departments were struggling and the company's technology and equipment was far behind that of our competitors. Overall the whole process was successful which resulted in minor department changes but management realized that there were some departments that needed better training and possibly new managers.

At staff meetings I come to realize that I needed to express my opinion and stick to my convictions. I work to support other females in our organization and work diligently to hire female managers at GreyStone. I have won the respect of the president/CEO and other male peers that serve on the Executive Team. They frequently seek me out to discuss ideas and to support their programs, and they support my ideas and programs as well.

I was invited to attend the Douglas County Leadership program. This is a nine-month program that introduces attendees to civic organizations in the community to educate them on volunteer opportunities in Douglas County. This program led to more recognition as a member of the leadership team of GreyStone Power Corporation.

In 2004, another Vice President at GreyStone Power Corporation and I were given the opportunity to attend NRECA's Management Internship Program. This six-week program is held at the University of Wisconsin each year. Participants must commit to attend the programs for two weeks at a time and are housed in housing on the campus. It is a tremendous privilege to have the opportunity to graduate from this program within the EMC arena. Through this program I added an even bigger network of friends and EMC pals.

I have talked about all the boards, promotions, schools and other opportunities that have come my way since graduating from college some 15 years ago. I owe many of these opportunities to my ABWA leadership roles and the wonderful friends and smart women that I have connected with. I joined this chapter several years after graduating from college. ABWA has provided me with many wonderful experiences and many career-enhancing opportunities that I never imagined would come to me.

Acting in leadership rolls in our local ABWA chapter gave me the self-confidence in my ability to lead and direct people. Nothing is impossible. Our chapter participates in many events in the community. We publicize our activities in the local newspaper and participate in the Mad Hatters Tea Party, sponsor scholarships, present fashion shows, career fairs and help with the annual Chili Cook-off and Taste for the Arts programs with the CAC. The list goes on and on. Douglas County knows that ABWA is alive and well in Douglasville. These events allow me to showcase my talents and grow lasting friendships.

Attending National ABWA Conferences played a role in helping me to acquire the self-confidence necessary for me to handle the role that I serve in my professional life. At one of the conferences, I attended a networking class. I purchased the program and presented it later to our chapter. Other classes that I attended focused on our attitudes and actions. It is important to keep a positive attitude in every aspect of our lives. We are held accountable for our actions and the image that we portray to others. I do programs at GreyStone Power and discuss with women the importance of protecting your image and dressing for success. One bad incident can destroy one's reputation in a second that has taken a lifetime to build.

Being named one of the Top Ten women in the nation is an awesome experience. I am ready to share my ABWA experience of growth and development with other women who do not yet know their true strength. I want to encourage women to reach for new heights and to join our ranks and keep ABWA in the headlines.

ABWA has been such a driving and motivating force in helping me to achieve my professional goals and dreams that I want to continue to mentor other young businesswomen as they climb up the corporate ladder. I cannot overestimate the influence ABWA has had in helping me to become a top executive at GreyStone Power and respected in the community for my accomplishments. I plan to continue to communicate the story of ABWA and the mission that was started nearly 70 years ago. As one of the Top Ten women of ABWA, I will be able to expand my circle of influence and assist more women in becoming successful in the business world.

Now I better understand what Eleanor Roosevelt meant. Through all my struggles to educate myself and to develop self esteem and self confidence, I must still stay true to the principles, work ethics and values that were taught to me in my youth. I understand and appreciate the value of friends and the importance of families in our lives. I must always continue to do the things I think I cannot do.

Epilogue

Serving as a member of ABWA and the "TOP TEN" group of women has been an awesome experience both in ABWA and within the community. Getting acquainted with this great group of ten women began at the National ABWA Conference in Greenville, North Carolina. After sharing our stories, we all agreed to begin a new phase on this journey that brought us together and to continue this experience by telling our stories in a book together. We are still making memories. Over the past year we held monthly conference calls to plan our strategies and to discuss ideas to each write a chapter for our book. This wild idea is about to become a reality.

After attending the ABWA Spring Conference in April, Ritchie Morris and I planned and organized an ABWA Leadership training program for Atlanta area ABWA members. The program was planned around ABWA and member responsibilities, officer duties, and some of the changes coming about within the organization. Nearly 60 members attended the event and it received great reviews.

The time has come for a new group of ABWA members to take our place as the 2009 Top Ten and to let the stars shine on them as they begin their year of glory. The 2008 group of ten women will join the ranks of the other Top Ten Women in the US. We will not fade away but will continue to shine and to make our mark within the ABWA circle of women. We will strive to carry the story of ABWA forward.

Diana Morales Taylor

Laura and Bonnie were having a margarita (I usually save my calories for food because I have been a diabetic since I was 18 years old) as we enjoyed our time together while compiling a list of speakers for the programs of the coming year of the Humble Artesian Chapter of ABWA. My cell phone kept ringing, but not recognizing the number or even the area code, I did not answer it. My cell phone rang again. This time it was my husband, who rarely calls, making sure that I had spoken to the "Ab Wah" woman who was looking for me. "Randy, don't worry, we've found each other and are getting our work done," I replied.

He retorted that I should get home soon because my son, David, and Mason, our 4-year old grandson, had unexpectedly dropped by. Seeing Mason and David are the highlights of my life. Although we've been married more than 40 years Randy and I have one son, and our son has only one son.

Because I'm a Puerto Rican Catholic, it's hard to imagine me as having one child. But much of that has to do with scoliosis, the curvature of the spine that was diagnosed when I was 12 years old living in Germany, and chronic back problems I have experienced all my life.

Immediately I told Bonnie and Laura that I had to scoot; we had done our work and now it was time to head home.

When I arrived home I was enthralled when little Mason greeted me with hugs, kisses, and big loud "Nanas." The phone rang; my husband picked it up and handed it to me. The woman on the other end of line was Robin, the national president of ABWA, and wanted to let me know that I had been selected one of the Top Ten Business Women of the Year for 2008. She had tried to call me on my cell phone while at the restaurant, but I had never picked up.

I was elated and starting jumping up and down. Little Mason was so excited he jumped right along with me. When I explained to my husband and son that I had been nominated by the chapter and won on a national level, they were duly impressed and just as excited as Mason. Once more I was on a journey about which I understood little and for which I had not planned. Two fellow ABWA sisters, Germaine Porche and Caroline Smith, had encouraged, coached and supported me in applying for this great honor. I had taken their advice, but really understood little about the honor and the process.

What most people don't realize is that there are so many kinds of "normal" in this wonderful world of ours. It is what makes us strong and makes us weak. When you grow up between cultures you learn that lesson at an early age. My job is about eliminating racism and empowering women. I am here because of a wonderful friend who heard of an opportunity and thought of me.

My career had been in corporate America. I had worked for more than 30 years in the roles of chief financial officer, chief operations officer and business owner in the fields of law, advertising, public relations, higher education, funeral home administration, community development and public accounting. Financially and professionally, I had achieved much and my reputation was one of getting things done. But, within me I felt emptiness, as if my purpose was not yet fulfilled. Though I am a goal setter, I tend to listen to my little inner voice and watch for life's signs about the big decisions.

I had chosen being a CPA as a career path because it was a quick route to a professional career that would provide a reliable, steady income for my family. However, after 25 years I was tired of making rich people richer, mostly at the expense of those who could not or did not have any choices in life.

As I listened to the stories of these wonderful rank and file employees, and heard their dreams for their children and their hope for the future, I knew that what I wanted to do was help these hardworking people learn what most of us know – how to earn a living using our talents and get our share of the abundance in this world.

I was born in Santurce, Puerto Rico to extremely traditional Latin parents. I was the oldest of three daughters, and we were brought up as proper young ladies – we did not talk about boys, money or careers. Therefore, in 1976 when I graduated from Florida State University with a degree in accounting, I did not think that I would be trailblazing a path normally followed by men.

Sometimes when I think back to the work environment I have seen since the 60s, it is difficult to believe that in only 40 years ago our society has grown so much. Though I have met an incredible number of characters in my career, the ones whom I remember best were those who became my "heroes."

My heroes were wonderful people who took the time to coach or mentor me about how "it really was" or how I needed to comport myself in any given situation. When ABWA asked to pick one person who was the best example of servant leadership, it was difficult for me. I have had so many wonderful men and women help, mentor and lead me. It was really hard to pick one, especially since we could not name a family member.

My wonderful husband of 40 years, Randy, is my best

friend and mentor. He really ranks up there; he taught so much about working in the male dominated world of public accounting. My father taught me how to survive in the work world of a different culture. My mother taught me what unconditional love is. But, perhaps the most selfless act of service and leadership to someone lesser that I have witnessed was exhibited to me by Betsy Cline of Columbus, Ohio in 1958.

You see at that time I was an 8-year old Puerto Rican girl who spoke only Spanish. Miss Cline was my third grade teacher. My father, a soldier in the US Army, had been transferred from Puerto Rico to Frankfurt, Germany and my sister and I were the only Spanish-speaking students in the American elementary school we attended. Every day Miss Cline moved seats into a supply room and taught me English while the rest of my class took German lessons. She had to develop worksheets for each day's lesson because there was no curriculum for her to use. I vividly remember one lesson where she had drawn a clothesline with little clothes that appeared to wave in the wind. That lesson focused on sun, wind, drying and washing clothes.

At the end of the school year Miss Cline asked my parents to meet with her. My timid mother, who never learned to speak English, begged that she not be made to attend the meeting. My father, an orphan with a third grade education and a GED he had earned while in the Army, came to school where Miss Cline have him a bibliography of books I was to read during the summer, preferably out loud. Every week of that summer my father took me to the library where the librarian and I checked off each book as I read them one by one. My mother listened to my reading even if she did not understand it.

This year I celebrate 30 years as a CPA. I have a BS in accounting, an MBA, and a passion for education that most people in Houston know about. How can I not pay it forward? By giving me the gift of language and never making me feel that I was less because I did not speak English, Miss Cline taught me to treat others and myself with deep respect and dignity.

Education was always important to me. I did well in my studies because I loved learning. I met my husband, Randy, when he and I were inducted into the National Honor Society in high school. Randy and I began seeing each other; our lives were really busy with studies, activities and college applications. By our senior year, Randy was president of the Honor Society and I was editor of our high school newspaper. Randy and I both received full college scholarships.

My parents did not allow me to date anyone, much less an American. As our relationship grew, Randy and I knew we needed to be together. One Saturday in mid-May 1968, I left my home with just my purse and nothing else. By July I was pregnant, without a job or a place to live. I was certainly down but I had had to fight to take care of myself all my life.

My father was both emotionally and physically absent from our lives. As the oldest of three daughters, I played the role of head of the family with my mother when Dad was stationed overseas. What I was facing in 1968 was just much greater in scope.

It was hard finding a job in Columbus, Georgia in 1968. I had great SAT scores but I could not type. I applied for a job at an insurance company that required aptitude testing. They were thrilled to tell me I had scored the highest of any applicant, yet I did not get the job because I could not pass the typing test. Not many jobs were open to women who couldn't type. Finally, I was hired by Southern Bell to be an information operator.

By September, Randy and I were married and six months later I gave birth to a wonderful baby boy, David. Although we were 18 years old, we did not give up our dream of education.

My family had returned to Puerto Rico in July where my dad was retiring from the Army. Randy and I focused on starting a life for our young family. Randy worked full-time as did until Southern Bell forced me to take a leave of absence in my seventh month of pregnancy.

Randy attended college full-time I managed our household – pinching every penny to ensure that we moved forward. Within seven years, both of us had earned our college undergraduate degrees. Randy and I became CPAs and he began his career in banking; I focused on public accounting. At the age of 49, I returned to school and earned an MBA. Before long our son, David, also earned his degrees and is now a registered architect here in Houston.

After much planning and hard work, I am now in my dream job as CEO of the YWCA in Houston, Texas. Our mission is eliminating racism and empowering women. Can you believe I get paid to do this? You can see why ABWA has become an extension of my work.

My Humble Artesian Chapter sisters have supported me in all my endeavors and I am hopeful that they feel I have reciprocated. My life's mission is to celebrate our dignity and humanity every day regardless of looks, shape, color, age, social status or beliefs. I hope that my service attitude will inspire others to follow in my footsteps.

I was a Rotarian for more than 20 years and their motto of "Service above self" was a daily inspiration for me. As I looked for ways to focus on my passion, doors began to open.

Right now my greatest personal and professional goal is to make the YWCA Houston the best affiliate of the YWCA USA and the greatest social service agency that serves women and minorities in Houston, Texas. Currently, I am the CEO of the YWCA Greater Houston. I began my employment here on June 1, 2004, based upon the recommendation of the local United Way agency when the Board of Directors was searching for an interim director. When I came here, the organization had less than four weeks of cash available, no prospects for additional funding in the near future and many contingent liabilities that could have easily put it out of business. Within four weeks the Board of Directors had offered the position permanently to me. The hard work began.

With an organization that was more than 96 years old, we had a rich history that was both a blessing and a challenge. We had to work with both internal and external stakeholders as we began the process of rebuilding our reputation and devising systems that would allow us to deliver excellent programs. Today we have more than $5 million of cash-on-hand and innovative, quality programs that make us highly sought after by other agencies and clients. We want to continue to build on these successes.

A lifelong learner, I am committed to continuing to grow my knowledge of the issues facing the social sector that impact our programs and service delivery. But my greatest desire is to bring to light the many issues that impact minorities and women based on both a philosophical and evidential viewpoint.

Writing has always been an important part of my life. I write in a journal often, if not daily. Though I have had articles published, my efforts have been casual and not greatly focused. In the Houston area I am known as a strong advocate for women's issues and I would like to use my experience in the corporate and non-profit world as a basis for my writing.

Women's empowerment and development have been the mainstays of both my professional and personal life for many years. When I was approached for membership into ABWA by Mary Howell, I was intrigued by the cross section of careers, professions and jobs that were represented within the chapter. Increasing the economic empowerment of women has been a personal goal of my adult life. Of course, membership in ABWA was a natural fit for me.

As a Hispanic female and first generation college graduate, the focus on education that ABWA exhibits firmly aligns with my personal commitment to the value of education.

At each meeting, the focus on educational development is clear. Whether it is the magazine, our speakers, or chapter fundraising to generate funds for women's scholarships, ABWA, as I do, understands that the quickest path to self sufficiency and resilience is education.

However, the greatest contributor by ABWA to my goals has been the wonderful support and encouragement that each member and the chapter collectively have shown me. I find the camaraderie and collegiality that my chapter sisters share with me to be instrumental in the success I have achieved. I am confident that when I engage the services of a fellow chapter member I will receive professional services, fair pricing, and outstanding customer service.

During my work as the program chair, I was able to bring to ABWA as speakers many of the outstanding women that I know in Houston. They provided major educational moments and opportunities to our membership. One such speaker was Jewel Smith.

Jewel is the Supplier Diversity Manager of CenterPoint Energy, a publicly-traded company headquartered in Houston. But even more important is her long history of involvement with the Houston Minority Business Council and Houston Women's Enterprise Council. Both of these initiatives focus on matching big publicly-traded businesses such as ExxonMobil, Chevron, AIG and Hewlett Packard with small businesses owned by women and minorities.

When Jewel Smith spoke to our chapter she facilitated our members' certifications as historically under-utilized businesses to allow them to participate in set aside programs. One of the women who participated has received work from Chevron and other large organization in the Houston area.

I have provided opportunities for members of ABWA to participate as vendors when the YWCA Greater Houston has needs for their services and they meet our purchasing guidelines. We have advertised employment opportunities available within our agency to the chapter membership.

The YWCA Greater Houston under my leadership has supported ABWA through sponsorships, collaborations and joint meetings whenever possible.

I became a member of ABWA about four years ago. Since then I have chaired the program committee and served as chapter vice-president, in addition to serving on the fundraising projects for three years and on the education committee. I am known within the chapter as someone who will lend a hand in any way at any time. I have also attended area council meetings and education trainings.

Because my membership with ABWA began almost at the same time as my employment with the YWCA and our agency was facing such monumental challenges, I have not been able to participate as fully in ABWA as I would like. Next year I plan to increase my participation in the leadership of the chapter since the YWCA Greater Houston is clearly on the road to organizational and financial stability.

I remain deeply committed to education. Although in order to maintain my license as a CPA I must attend 40 hours of continuing education every year, I usually have more than 60.

One of the focuses of the YWCA is to provide training and education to all affiliates. I also have instituted a policy within our organization that each year as part of each employee's performance appraisal, she and her supervisor will create a list of training goals for the year.

Katreena Hayes-Wood

A New Beginning

It began with a prayer.

It was a prayer for the strength to stick with the decision I had made to leave an alcoholic husband; to start a new and better life; to be able to support myself and my two young sons; to have enough self-confidence to make my life work and to somehow, some way find the spark that used to be me.

My career really began the day I decided to leave an abusive relationship, take my sons, Keaton and Kalab, both of whom were under the age of three, and move to Phoenix, Arizona to start over. I was fortunate because three years earlier I had lived in Phoenix and worked for ESP Personnel, a permanent and temporary employment agency. The owner of the company, Ann Freedle, told me the day I left that if I ever needed a job to call her. So, when I arrived in

Phoenix on Sunday, January 14, 1990 I called Ann. By the following Monday I had a wonderful outside sales position with AppleOne, the company that had bought ESP Personnel the year before.

My conversation with Ann was fairly straightforward, and without saying a word she understood my divorce. As is most often the case, the people around me already knew I was in an abusive relationship, even thought I worked diligently to hide that very fact. But Ann knew the truth, and she also knew that I'd be an honest, hardworking and energetic employee on whom she could count. I never let her down and my career began to soar.

I experienced some bumps in the road along my career path, but nothing that my growing confidence and newly found success couldn't handle. I discovered that I was an awesome mother with an ability to connect with my boys and to really be there for them. I learned that I was stronger and smarter than I had ever realized and I knew, beyond a shadow-of-a-doubt, that my "bad times" were over.

Some of the challenges I navigated around included a difficult relationship and break-up, and leaving AppleOne to pursue a different career opportunity and later being laid-off from that position due to corporate cut backs. But in November of 1991 I landed a dream position with DeVry University in Career Services. That job changed my life.

DeVry was the perfect career move for me. It taught me about professionalism; it challenged my career skills, and honed my creative, idea-oriented mind. It was also a job that provided pure fun, where I discovered that I really had the power to make a significance impact on the lives of others. I continued to work at DeVry for more than five years, during which I was promoted to Assistant Director of Career Services. My two years in management taught me about diplomacy and the importance of loyalty and being true to myself, including being strong enough to stand up for what I believed in and what I stood for.

Because of all that I learned, DeVry was my testing ground. It was the incubator for who I would become, personally and professionally. It wasn't always easy, it wasn't always fun, but I knew that each day I had an opportunity to make a difference, and even now I am still extremely proud of what I was able to achieve. Some of those accomplishments included a young man who came to my office one evening literally on the verge of suicide. My boss, Molly Abt, came in to my office and asked me to talk to the troubled young man. When Molly explained that he was suicidal, I told her that I simply was not qualified to help him. She disagreed and told me, "Katreena, of all the people who work for me, you have the most heart. Tonight I need you to use your heart to help this young man."

So, I agreed to help. I said a quick prayer and hoped I would find the words. I listened, asked questions and together we made a list of what he needed to do the next day, the next week and the entire semester to accomplish the goals we had set out for my new, young friend. Two years later he graduated with a 3.8 GPA and a job that paid $40,000 per year. He was one of my first successes helping others with their careers and he taught me that loving and caring for people will always have a positive impact on their lives.

Two life significant events occurred while I was at DeVry: I met and married my best friend, Jeff Wood, and I took a Spiritual Mastery class. If DeVry was the incubator for my career, the Spiritual Mastery class was the launching pad!

The Transition

I was fascinated by what I learned about myself during the Spiritual Mastery class. Because I've always been a reasonably good student, I took my assignments seriously. The first one, I remember, is that we were to create a document that encompassed all the things we wanted to accomplish in our lives. I was excited to work on this task and proudly showed our instructor my eighteen-page text the following week. With a broad smile on his face, he asked me to tell him in one sentence what my eighteen pages meant. "What," I croaked, "How do you expect me to summarize my eighteen pages into one sentence?"

My instructor placed his strong hand on my shoulder and wisely replied, "Katreena, if you cannot tell me what you stand for in one sentence, what good will eighteen pages do?"

Then he continued to explain to the rest of our class, "What you're working on is your personal mission statement, like Nike's marketing tag line, '*Just do it.*' You also need to have a phrase, or a one-liner that sums up who you are and what you stand for."

The following week I returned to class with my personal mission statement in hand. I am proud to say I still live by it today. My personal mission statement is: To touch lives in a positive way … every day!

And I do!

Every day when I wake up and I walk out the door, I seize the opportunity to be a positive force for others and to extend that attitude to everyone I meet. People often ask me if I am in fact always so positive and happy, and I have to tell you that yes, I am. Being happy, in my opinion, is a choice you make. Being positive, having a good attitude, and creating joy in your life are also deliberate choices.

The other thing I discovered in my Spiritual Mastery Class is that when the universe decides it's time for you to make a move, whether in your career or your personal life, and you don't get that message and make that change, then the universe will make it for you. Now don't get me wrong here, I'm not talking about some magical or religious hocus pocus. What I'm talking about is the soft voice of your own intuition that quietly whispers that it's time for a change and we, with our busy lives and schedules, don't consciously hear that message. What we do is ignore the message. Well, I heard the message and it scared me. It was time to leave DeVry.

And so that is how I came to be self-employed. On some level I knew that if I didn't leave DeVry then that I would be forced to leave at some point in the future. Coincidently, this pivotal time occurred while my son Keaton was having a difficult time in school — so much so that we needed to make a decision to put him in a special education contained classroom. What that meant is that he needed more than special help with his classes a few times a week, but needed daily assistance to succeed in school. In my heart I knew that Keaton also needed more of me.

In January 1997 I started Career Services Network. I was terrified at the prospect of starting from scratch. "Haven't I done this before?" I thought. "Haven't I already been down this path?"

The answer was, "yes." I would remind that I had started from scratch before, and that yes I had made it work, because I had to, for me and for my children. My husband Jeff was supportive. His support meant more to me that a pat on the back and a vote of confidence; it meant change and struggle and sacrifice. Jeff began working 60 hours per week to make up the difference in the initial loss of income. I cashed out my 401K to give us a cushion to provide a safety net for emergencies. As I look back on those times I realize they were harrowing, they were horrifying, and I wouldn't exchange one minute of one day for the experience, or for the lessons.

What I got was the freedom to be there for my kids who thought they had a stay-at-home mom. At first I took whatever work I could get, like employment search, research and placement. The money was inconsistent, but decent.

Introduced to ABWA

At the same time I started Career Services Network, I attended my first American Business Women's Association meeting. My good friend, Dr. Barbara Roe-Snow, invited me to attend, adamant that I needed to get more involved in networking which she promised would help me to grow my business. In April 1997, I joined the Mai Ta Kola chapter of ABWA, in Phoenix, Arizona. The president, Candace Ryan, ("Candy") welcomed me with open arms, it seemed, because I felt connected to her immediately. She was friendly and confident, someone I wanted to get to know.

Right away, she had me involved with the chapter and we became fast friends.

My friendship with Candy has been one of the pinnacles of my life. She is my dearest friend and confidant, someone for whom I have great respect, in whom I trust, and who has always encouraged me to be and do my personal best.

In the years that followed, my involvement in ABWA taught me about teamwork and leadership when I helped with the ABWA National Convention that was held in Phoenix and when I helped to start a new, much needed chapter. In November 1999 the Arrowhead Millennium chapter was chartered with sixty new members and a slate of officers that included me, Dr. Roe-Snow, Carol Cousins and Phoenix newcomer, Klissa Rueschoff who was from Kansas City.

In 2001, I served as our chapter's president and Candy was my vice-president. It was during that year that I found my professional voice and was encouraged by Dr. Roe-Snow to add public speaking to my career repertoire. I was also honored as our chapter's Woman of the Year in 2001. And if things weren't moving fast enough, my career focus was beginning to shift.

Strive For Students is Born

Two years after joining ABWA, I decided I wanted to help my eighth-grade son Keaton, and his special education friends to make career choices and teach them how to be successful in the workplace. For ideas and support, I approached a friend at DeVry, Mary James. Mary was the business administrator at DeVry. She was smart and in my opinion possessed real business savvy. I shared with Mary my idea to help Keaton and his friends with their careers. She very wisely asked me, "If you're going to spend all this time developing a program for your son and his friends, why don't you spend the extra time, do some market research and see if there is a viable need and start a business?"

It didn't take me long to determine that I would love to develop a company that offered programs to help students who were undecided about their careers to discover an ideal career field and help them to develop the tools and skills to be successful in the workplace. Mary liked the idea, too, and we agreed to become business partners.

We had a strong team, Mary with her business administration background and me with my career development experience. We named our company over coffee on a Saturday afternoon and STRIVE (Student Training and Resources for Individualized Vocational Employment) was born. We later renamed it Strive For Students.

In early 1999, Strive For Students was fortunate to add another team member to our fold, Marcia Maish. Marcia was a retired English teacher with more than eighteen years experience in education and several years of marketing background. Marcia provided the educational curriculum and presentation piece that we so desperately needed.

With our team assembled, we began the arduous task of defining who might need the student career development program services we offered, who wanted those services, and just how much they were worth. We piloted a career development program we called Discovery Career Camp at the T.J. Pappas high school for homeless youths. Though we received rave reviews from the students and the faculty, we also learned a lot about our program, program content, curriculum, and teaching methods. We also uncovered more answers from our market research. After eighteen months of hard work what we found is that the students that were underserved are those is the middle, not the honors students or the special education/special needs like those at T.J. Pappas.

Apparently there was already a wealth of services and people available to help them with their career choices and challenges. Thus began a redefining of our program that focused on average students and their career development needs.

It was at this point that we lost Marcia Maish as the demands on her personal life and the pull from her other, more financially advantageous career pursuits made it necessary for her to move past. However, Mary and I continued to redefine Strive For Students.

Also, during this time I began the research for my first career development book, *Help! I Need a Job, the Desktop Guide to the Perfect Interview,* which was published in May 2002.

The Bumpy Road to Success

With a renewed and revised curriculum, we were ready to launch our marketing campaign. We decided to officially launch our new program in September 2001. We had a Discovery Career Camp schedule for September 11. I don't have to remind you what happened on that world-changing day, but I can tell you we knew there was no doubt that launching a new career development program was the least of our concern. In the shadow of 9-11 we decided to wait until January 2002 to think about the future direction of Strive For Students and what we wanted to do with our new program.

The next year included a string of events, not all negative, but all having a significant impact on the growth of Strive For Students. First, Mary and I approached my grandmother, Grace Hayes for a loan of $10,000 to help market and grow our business. Grandma granted us the loan that included a wish for luck and vote of confidence. We used our new source of funding to buy advertising promoting upcoming workshops that we hosted at local area high schools. Our evening Discover Career Camp classes were well attended and we felt positive about our progress.

It was during this time that my good friend Candy introduced me to her step-daughter in Grand Junction, Colorado. Jenny ran a foster home for girls in Grand Junction and was looking for ways to help them transition from foster care to independent, adult living because when a youth turns eighteen he or she is no longer served by the foster care program and is expected to "graduate" to adulthood.

Jenny recommended I contact a woman, a caseworker, who worked for the foster care program in Colorado. Her name was Rosalyn, and she referred me to the state director of the Chaffee Program, a program that focuses on transitioning youths in the State of Colorado's foster care program to independent adult living.

Strive For Students landed its first major account. In February 2002, Mary and I traveled to Denver, Colorado to deliver our three-day Discover Career Camp for 20 students in the State of Colorado's Chafee Program.

Prior to our departure, Mary and I were faced with the most difficult decision possible regarding our business partnership. We had promised each other that if either of us ever wanted to dissolve our partnership, we would do so with no hard feelings. We believed that our friendship was important — more important than our business. Just weeks before we left for Colorado, Mary told me that she needed to bow out of Strive For Students. We had both been struggling with the different ways we conducted business. Both of us were strong and driven businesswomen, with differing personalities and ways of accomplishing our goals. Mary was cautious and methodical, making sure that all details were attended to; I, on the other hand, was the risk-taking, sales person. I impatiently pushed Mary to do things out of her comfort zone and she cautiously held me back to the point of frustration! We were also two good friends, with a similar vision who were tormented on how to take the business to the next level. Finally, one evening we tearfully decided it was time to part ways as business partners.

Mary traveled with me to Denver to deliver our program, but before we left we dissolved our business partnership and Mary signed on as a consultant for Strive For Students. When we returned from Denver, Mary went to work for a local non-profit and I continued to build Strive For Students.

Going Solo

I'd like to pause here to say something about building a business. It really does take five to seven years to build a successful one. What nobody told me was that during that time I would face every internal demon I have ever encountered! I faced insecurity and doubt. I wondered and worried over the abilities that up to this point I'd taken for granted — abilities like creativity and organization. I questioned my capacity to bring my vision into reality, and so did my husband, Jeff. I dealt with guilt, because everyone wanted a piece of me and there never seemed to be enough pieces to go around! I ranted and raved and shook my fist to the heavens, cursing God for giving me this crazy dream. I cried, I wallowed and I felt downright lousy. I speculated on my intelligence. I mean let's face it, how smart could I be to give up a cushy job, earning a decent salary where I only had to work 40 hours per week? Yeah, I experienced the gamut of emotions. Going solo wasn't all it was cracked up to be, and yet it was what I wanted and truthfully what I really needed to be successful.

If you asked me if I would I do it again, I'd tell you yes!

Yes! Because as difficult as it was, there were other times that I wanted to burst with joy because what I was doing felt so right. With each passing day I came to realize that this work I do is MY WORK. I couldn't deny that my work was making a difference. But most of all, I realized that my dream was my work and that my work was my dream.

New Horizons

Shortly after parting ways with Mary, I began to work with the Native American community through the Workforce Investment Act program doing Work Readiness Training. My first big client was the Gila River Indian Community. They had a summer youth employment program and needed a trainer to teach work readiness skills to youth ages 14 to 21. It was a perfect venue for me and an incredible instrument for Gila River.

My first day, I went home in tears, certain that I had lost my touch. Sure that my ability to connect with my workshop attendees had disappeared, I cried all the way home. I kept questioning my skills and the workshop materials. I slumped into the house and told my husband Jeff I needed to start looking for a real job because the kids hated me. As I cried, feeling remarkably sorry for myself, I wailed, "I'm tired of being ambitious. I just want to be a minimum wage, fast food worker."

Jeff took my hands in his, looked into my eyes and gently replied, "It's going to be okay. Today you can be whatever you want to be, and remember tomorrow is a brand new day."

The next day at the end of my class I stopped by the office of the program coordinator, Teresa Masayesva. With a huge smile on her face she told me the students loved me, "Katreena, the students just love you. I don't know what you did, but you really connected with them. Thanks."

My business has really taken off. It's taken me ten long years of hard work with a solid product that's tried and true. During those years I have worked as an educational consultant to help school districts write strategic and tactical plans for program planning and growth; I've planned and hosted corporate functions, like the executive retreat I did for the Ft. McDowell Indian Community's tribal council and business community leadership. I've delivered hundreds of presentations ranging from my popular Dream*Builder*© Workshop, Stress Busters, and Building Your Authentic Self, to corporate programs like Bringing Fun Back to the Workplace, What's Your Color at Work?, and Building Strong and Trusting Work Relationships. I've developed programs, like GET — Girls Exploring Technology — a gender equity program to help girls explore the diverse fields of technology to programs to help youth and young adults expand their knowledge of financial planning and time management. I've also volunteered hundreds of hours for student organizations, school districts, and career expos, and I serve on the board of directors for Bosom Buddies of Arizona, a support organization for people with breast cancer.

There is so much more that I have done and that I plan to continue to do, develop, and deliver. All of my dreams and aspirations have come from a philosophy that can be summed up by the answer to a question that my dear friend Teresa from Gila River asked me nearly six years ago when I first started working for them. Teresa asked me what it was I did that made the students like me so much. I replied with the only answer that has ever really made sense: That when you love people, that when you really care for them, they always come around. You cannot fake loving something; you cannot pretend to enjoy something because one thing I know for sure is that the truth will always bear itself out.

A Philosophy for Life

"We are all here for a reason and our only job is to figure out why. The way we do that is by defining our gifts. Our gifts are our natural strengths, abilities, skills, talents, our values and interests and those things for which we are profoundly passionate. Then we are called to use those very gifts to serve humanity. By serving others we will find our purpose in life, our career and we will make the world a better place." (Katreena Hayes-Wood)

I believe that I was born to deliver the message above. Every time I teach a class, deliver a speech, or have an opportunity to talk to someone about his or her purpose in life I share this philosophy. Reread that paragraph, let it resonate with you, let the words gently wash over you; feel them, really absorb them and you will find that there is a strong and deeply significant message there for you too.

My greatest gift is the ability to help people discover their purpose in life.

I believe that we are all here to learn to love better. We all have the gift of love; we are born with the ability to love. The greatest gift we give the world is to love ourselves, for when we love ourselves we extend who we are out to others in a loving way, a non-confrontational, non-competitive way and we bridge the gap between ourselves and all those with whom we come into contact.

Every day we have an opportunity to make a conscious choice to live a good life, to have a positive impact on others and to make the world a better place. As Gandhi once said, "Be the change you wish to see in the world."

Make the world a better place, because you can! Every thought you think creates your future. If you think positive thoughts, you create a positive future for you and everyone around you too. If you carry negativity in your heart and soul, you cannot help but attract those very kinds of people into your life. Change your thoughts and you will change your life. Every day is a new beginning, a new opportunity to begin the life you have always wished and imagined you could have. Start by defining who you are; decide to have a strong, moral character, a positive attitude and search for the spark that is you and give it to the world. And start today!

Being a Top Ten

When Robin Necci, 2007 ABWA National President, contacted me and told that I had been awarded the honor of the American Business Women Association's Top Ten I was thrilled. I mean, who wouldn't be? It is the highest honor they can bestow on a fellow ABWA member. More thrilling than winning the award for me was meeting my nine fellow "Tenners" at the national convention in North Carolina in September 2007. What an amazing group of women.

During the national convention I had the opportunity to get to know each of my Top Ten sisters better; here's what I learned about each them that I'd like to share with you:

• Julie Kangas is such a delight. She is kind and soft spoken, with that underlying ability to be strong and firm in her convictions. She is a gentle giant of a leader and will honorably serve ABWA at the helm as our 2008 American Business Woman of ABWA.

• There is Tina Ackles, the youngest of our group, who is an amazingly talented and interesting young woman, a single mother with a passion for life and service to her country that is humbling. She is dynamic and strong and so very, very fun to spend time with.

• Janet Deyette is the oldest of our group and showed up at convention with a cast on her foot, in a wheelchair, and a can-do attitude that's hard to beat. She was so friendly and welcomed everyone she met with open arms. She has an incredible ability to work magic with numbers and details, too, which I greatly admire (and envy).

• Rebecca Pulliam Francis is poised and has an appeal that is endearing. She embodies servant leadership with her work and should be commended for the 200-page dissertation, just completed this year. She also has put her life and career on hold to help her sister this year.

• Christina Robinson Grochett is simply a beautiful woman. It's obvious when you look at her to see her outward beauty, but when you get to know her you realize that she has that rare ability to be truly beautiful on the inside and out. She is kind and smart and so very giving.

• Richie Morris can best be described as "dynamic"! She has such a presence that you notice her when she walks into a room, and she has a commanding and vibrant way of conducting herself. She exudes confidence and yet she is approachable and easy to talk to.

• Diana Morales Taylor is a wonder. She has overcome

obstacles that would stagger an average person and she is anything but average. She comes from humble beginnings and has taken her gentle upbringing and used that to serve the women in the Houston area.

• Marcita Scharnhorst embodies the saying "dynamite comes in small packages." As I sit here looking at her picture from the *Women in Business* magazine I remember how confident she is and her smile is a quick reminder of the humor that lies beneath the exterior of the strong, resilient women.

• Christine Wright is quite simply a burst of energy. She could, no doubt, do anything she set her mind to. She has accomplished so much already for someone her age. She is driven and focused and has done an amazing job as a lawyer and public servant about which she is understandably very proud.

It would be easy to write pages and pages about these amazing women, but more important than writing about them is be the opportunity to get to know them, to spend time with them and to serve with them, shoulder-to-shoulder on a project. This book has been such a privilege.

When we traveled to the ABWA National Conference in North Carolina in the fall of 2007 we, as Top Ten, were charged with the task of writing a three-minute speech, focusing on three key points: (1) Someone that we were not related to, who had made a significant impact on our career; (2) servant leadership and, (3) how we intended to use our year as Top Ten to "pay it forward."

The speech was to be delivered at the Woman of the Year luncheon on Saturday. As a professional speaker, writing my speech was extremely difficult for me and as my husband so lovingly declared, "I'm going to North Carolina to hear your speech because I've never heard you say anything in three minutes and I want to be witness to that rare occasion."

For the record, and for a shocker to all those folks who know me, I came in two seconds under my three-minute mark. My mother, Kleo Goforth; stepfather, Dr. Phillip Goforth; husband, Jeff and best friend Candy Ryan were there for me, as well as several ABWA sisters from Arizona — Diane Walters, 1980 Top Ten; Janet Maxwell, Phoenix Metropolitan Council Chairperson, and Julie Brown, Arrowhead Millennium chapter's vice president. Their support meant the world to me.

Candace Ryan is the person I chose as the one person whose support has made a significant impact on my career. I'd like to take this opportunity to personally thank her for her treasured friendship and the many hours of support and listening, especially during the times I needed a friendly boost – you know what I'm talking about, Candy!

My entire career has been one of servant leadership. I believe that I was born to serve and help others to discover their purpose in life. I appreciate the recognition of this life-long pursuit from ABWA as a 2008 Top Ten.

As my charge to pay it forward during my tenure as a 2008 Top Ten, I plan to accomplish this by launching ABWA chapters on high school campuses. As I explained in my three-minute Top Ten speech, as an educational consultant I have a huge network to draw from in Arizona. In addition, Dr. John Mulcahy, Director of the Career and Technical Education program for the Peoria Unified School District, has agreed to pilot the ABWA on high school campuses program in his district.

Paying it forward is a concept that Dr. Mulcahy exemplifies in his professional life on a daily basis. If I could embody the gifts of just one individual it would be Dr. Mulcahy whose work ethic and passion for making a difference in the lives of the teachers and students he serves is worthy of the highest praise. I would be honored to achieve just a fraction of what he has accomplished in his career. He is a man who has defined all of his life's gifts and who uses those very gifts every day to make the world a better place.

A Final Thought

Life is a gift. We are charged as children of this planet to learn to love one another more and to serve humanity in an effort to make the world a better place. We are all gifted and it is never too late to open the gift of your life. Success is not measured by the things you accomplish, but by the lives you touch using your gifts. Remember, we are all here for a reason and our only job is to figure out why. Define your gifts, use your gifts and somehow, someway find the spark that is YOU and make the world a better place.

Christine F. Wright

Throughout my life I have had obstacles come in the way of attaining my goals. I have had to accept short term setbacks in order to have the opportunity to move forward. Sometimes a setback turned into a learning experience, which I was able to use later on in life.

I have had many people who have influenced and supported me throughout my life. The most important person is my mother. I have been very fortunate to have a mother who allowed me to grow, make my own decisions and, on occasion, suffer the consequences of those decisions when things went wrong.

Since I was a small child, she always told me that I would go to college. It was not a matter open for discussion. My mother never went to college, and did not start working until I was about 11 years old. My father only has an A.S. degree. Although I didn't, my mother knew the importance of an education.

Eventually, I was 18 years old, married and working full time. My husband joined the Army and left for basic training a week after we were married. I joined him at his Army post in Georgia a few months later. While I knew I wanted to go to college, that goal seemed very far away. I had to work full time to help support us, and while most of the other wives I met only had the goal of having children, I would not give up the aspiration of a college education. I worked various jobs during those years, including bank teller and salesperson. After my husband's commitment to the Army was over, we moved back to Florida.

My relationship began to unravel, yet even while my marriage was falling apart, my mother pushed me to start college classes. By the time I was 22, I had divorced and had started taking courses part-time at community college. My husband had run us into a lot of debt, and I was trying to pay some of that off, support myself, and go to college. I was working full-time and some semesters took a full-time course load in the evening. Fortunately, my parents were paying my tuition.

I started college in 1987, part-time at first and then most semesters I was taking classes full-time in the evening while working full-time during the day. I was working for a national bank and started looking at what career options there were available in that industry. My goal was to get a bachelor's degree in Business Administration/Financing and continue working in the banking industry. As I continued my studies, I noticed that there were not a great many women in upper management. I also realized that while working in a large corporate situation had its advantages, I didn't believe that I would enjoy that type of career.

When I finally received my associate's degree in 1989, I transferred to a four-year university to get my bachelor's degree. At the same time I was re-evaluating my career options. It wasn't easy working full time and going to college. I needed a job that would allow me to take classes during the day, because the university did not have a comprehensive night program and it would have taken years to complete my bachelor's degree. I realized that I would need a job where I could take classes during the day.

One of the crazy things I did — and there have been many — is quit my job at the bank, without having a new job to go to. Fortunately, I was living with my brother in a condominium my parents owned. I knew I would not be evicted, since the only other option would be moving back in with them.

It was actually a customer at the bank who gave me the idea to bartend and I realized I could have a job that I could work nights and get paid to have fun. I spend the next two and half years finishing my bachelor's degree and working as a bartender. I was able to get a job at a popular nightclub, and because the hours were late, I learned not to schedule any classes before 10:00 a.m. My manager always worked around my school schedule, which changed each semester, and gave me extra days off during exams. It was so helpful working somewhere where I enjoyed the work and had a supportive management and co-workers.

I had always thought that I would pursue a degree beyond a bachelor's degree, but I did not decide to pursue a law degree until I had finished my associate's degree. After completing my bachelor's degree, I went to Germany for the summer and ended up staying there for one and a half years. My mother is from Germany from a small island called Sylt, which is in the North Sea on the Danish border. We had visited there a few times since I was little. Sylt is German tourist destination and is very busy during the summertime.

I had taken some German classes in college, always wanting to learn the language, and my family arranged a job for me to waitress during the summer season. It was a challenge at first, because with only two semesters of German, I had a hard time communicating. The kitchen staff was always amused at my attempts to write out special orders, since most of them were in German, but with English grammar.

After working that summer, I moved to Hamburg and enrolled in German classes. As a child, I was frustrated that my cousins in Germany had to learn English in school, but I had no opportunity to learn another language, let alone German. I was not able to take German classes until my last two years of college. Being able to live in Germany and continue learning the language, which I must say is easier when you have no choice but to speak it, was a personal goal of mine. I spent about seven months in Hamburg. I then worked another summer on Sylt at a different restaurant.

I really enjoyed living in Germany. I was able to get closer to my family there, especially my grandmother. I lived with her during both summers and we still keep in touch today. I go over to visit as often as I can. I also keep in touch with my cousins and we try to visit with each other each year.

After I returned to the U.S., I applied to law schools again. I was thrilled when I received my acceptance to St. Thomas University School of Law in Miami. I had applied to schools in other states, but was happy that I could stay close to my family while in law school.

Law school was challenging. My first year was the first time in my life that I did not work while going to school. I received a fellowship in my second year to work at Greater Miami Legal Services. I worked two semesters there in my second year and third year of school. Over the summers I took temporary jobs to pay the bills. Since there were three law schools in the greater Miami area, it was difficult to find a paying summer clerk position.

I was also active in student organizations on campus. During my second year I was a representative to student government and Lt. Governor of Resolutions for our ABA Law Student Division Circuit. During my third year I was more adventurous, taking on also the duties of Treasurer of my law fraternity chapter and Vice President for Entertainment of the Entertainment and Sports Law organization. It was a very hectic year trying to complete projects for the various organizations and keeping up with my studies.

During my last semester of law school, my mother was diagnosed with breast cancer. That summer studying for the bar exam was very tough. I was studying for the exam and my mother was getting her radiation treatments. Since she was a business owner, she did not have the option of taking a lot of time off. Her business partner also had a family member who was diagnosed with Stage 4 cancer that spring. It was not a happy time for any of us. I took my bar review course on Monday through Thursday and worked in the store on Friday so my mother could stay home and rest and her partner could help her family.

After the bar exam, I visited my family in Germany for four weeks. I knew once I started working I would probably not have the chance to travel there for a few years. Since Florida's bar results come out in mid-September, I knew I would not likely get a job interview before the results were posted. Before leaving for Germany, I had prepared my resume and had requested the career service's dean to send in my resume if she saw a job posting that she though I would be interested in. While I was in Germany, my school's career services department had faxed my resume to a firm that had sent in a job posting.

When I returned from Germany, I received a call from the firm requesting an interview. I ended up having to schedule the interview on the same day that bar results were posted. Before I went to the interview, I was able to go online and check the bar results. I was so excited when I found out I had passed. I went to the interview later that day and got the job. Although the employer was interested in the bar results, the fact that I was fluent in German is what got me the position. I had never expected to get job based on my language ability. I had learned German in order to be able to speak with my family.

When I returned home that evening, my family was anxiously awaiting to find out whether I had obtained the job. They did not know that bar results had also been posted that day. The look on my parents' faces when I told them that not only had I gotten the job, but that I had also passed the bar exam, was priceless.

The job also meant a move to the west coast of Florida. I settled into my new apartment and began work. It was not easy being somewhere new, where I didn't know anyone. The law firm was small, with only two other attorneys. It took awhile to adjust, but since my family was only two hours away, I did visit them often.

Although I had a law degree, I knew that there was much more I needed to learn about the practice of law. Also, although I was fluent in German, I still had to improve my writing skills and comprehension. The senior partner at the firm worked with me to improve my writing skills. I also attended seminars on the various areas of law that I practiced. While attorneys are required to take continuing education classes, I have usually taken more hours than have been required.

I enjoyed my work, but after being so active in law school in the various organizations, I missed that interaction. About a year after I moved, I got involved in the local realtors' association. One of my practice areas was real estate law, and this enabled me to market my services. I also participated on various committees doing various fundraising projects. I also started to become active in the local bar association.

After working at the law firm for four and half years, I made the decision to open my own firm. I could not have accomplished that without the support of my family. They not only supported my decision, but helped me set up my new office. At different times, each of my parents actually worked at the office when I needed them. My brother and father set up the computer network and my brother is only a phone call away whenever we have problems. My sister designed the print ads we use.

Shortly after I opened my own firm, I was introduced to ABWA. When I attended my first meetings I felt that I had found that certain something that had been missing. This was an amazing group of women, each supportive of each other and the mission of the organization. ABWA has helped me to learn more about business through the guest speakers we have at each monthly meeting and through my fellow chapter members. My fellow members have become friends and have always been available with advice and support when I needed it.

I was honored when my chapter elected me President after I had been a member for two years. I served two years as chapter President and have also served on various committees. I have enjoyed the work that our chapter does and the various fundraising events we hold. Through attending the many council, district and annual conferences, I have met more amazing women. I have also had the opportunity to take various business courses, which have helped me operate my firm. Because I had decided to pursue a law degree, I did not take many business courses. Now that I have my own firm, I realized that I needed to learn more about running a business, managing my employees and marketing my services.

ABWA has provided resources to meet those needs and more. My chapter members have always been willing to give me advice and encouragement. I have also expanded my market through the networking opportunities through my chapter and the organization.

In addition to my activities with ABWA, I have also been active with our local bar association and am currently mentoring a high school student. Through the local bar association I have been active the last five years in helping to coordinate the High School Mock Trial competition. Each year I have the opportunity to watch high school students conduct trials during the competition and I am always amazed at how well prepared and poised they are. As a mentor, I am involved in my student's life and helping her achieve her goal of obtaining a college education. She amazes me at how well she has dealt with the obstacles that she has had in her life and her dream to go to college. Having had a family that encouraged and supported me throughout my education, I enjoy being able to pass that encouragement and support on.

When I found out that I had been named one of the 2008 Top Ten of ABWA, I was honored. When we were asked to speak about the person who had supported and inspired us throughout our endeavors other than our family, I realized that I had not had one person, but many. While my family has always been there for me, I did not have that one person who was pivotal in my life. Throughout my education I had many professors who helped along the way, whether it was by giving advice about writing a paper or just explaining the material when I didn't understand. I have had bosses who arranged my schedule around my classes, gave me time off for exams, and encouraged me to continue my studies.

My friends have also been there for me and supported me along the way. I have a few friends that have been with me for over 25 years. We have been through all the ups and downs in all of our lives. Whenever I needed that shoulder to lean on or just to get away from everything, they were there for me. I have been very fortunate in the support that I have had throughout my life.

I want to pass that support and encouragement along. As a 2008 Top Ten I was asked to give my speech again at an ABWA Spring Conference. I have met women who have been faced with various challenges, especially in their careers. I want to let everyone know that they need to take every opportunity they have to learn and achieve something new — be it a new skill or a college degree. Whatever it is, you can attain it. Do not let anyone tell you, you cannot.

Each of us will face challenges in life that will cause us to detour off the path we want to go. I hope that I can encourage others that no matter what obstacle you encounter to face it, and take the opportunity to learn something new. You never know what skill or knowledge you have that will light the path to help you along the way.

Epilogue

My year as a Top Ten has been an interesting and challenging one. I have remained active in the various organizations that I am involved with, including ABWA.

The current economic situation has hit Southwest Florida hard, which has required me to adjust my practice areas in order to meet my clients' changing needs.

I attended two of ABWA's Spring Conferences and met other ABWA members who have also had to adjust their career paths to meet these challenging times. Talking with other members from around the country has inspired me about our ability to adjust to the detours that come our way and how the support you need is as close as the member next to you.

CPSIA information can be obtained at www.ICGtesting.com
Printed in the USA
LVOW102010241111

256304LV00001B/193/P

9 781881 276098